THE TRANSFORMATIVE EFFECT OF YOUTH SPORTS

THE TRANSFORMATIVE EFFECT OF YOUTH SPORTS:

Forging an intentional path towards enriching children's lives through sports

JASON KERRICK

PUBLISHED BY:
Jones Media Publishing
YourBookBlueprint.com

ISBN-10: 1522747079

ISBN-13: 978-1522747079

First Edition: December 2015

DEDICATION

This book is dedicated to Jen, Connor and Kennedy,
who inspire me to strive to be better every day.

ACKNOWLEDGEMENTS

I would like to thank all of my former teachers, coaches, teammates and players that I've coached who I have learned so many lessons from over the years. I would like to also thank Jeremy Jones for helping me to make my dream of one day writing a book become a reality through his guidance and support that led to this book being successfully launched. Thanks to my brother for the countless hours of practice as kids that further developed our love for sports and my sister for putting up with the both of us. I appreciate the culture that my parents created by enrolling us in any sport that we wanted and taking us to numerous games over the years that led to many great memories. Thank you to my kids, Connor and Kennedy, who inspire me to want to keep working to be a better person. Most importantly, thanks go out to my wonderful wife for being so supportive to me during my countless hours of work on this book.

CONTENTS

INTRODUCTION

Youth sports, which once provided so much fun and joy for generations of children, have now morphed into a big business that is barely recognizable when compared to the experience of previous generations. It's evolved to the point where youth sports have become more about benefitting people other than the children. Misguided motives of parents, coaches and league administrators, have taken a toll on participation in youth sports. Some horror stories have made national news detailing parents fighting amongst one another, verbal and physical attacks on umpires/referees and other stories of head-scratching behavior. These headlines might make the purist wonder how far off track youth sports have gone? We need to simplify and bring back the purity, innocence and the fun so future generations can continue to benefit from sports on the way to becoming contributing members of society.

As a lifetime lover of sports, coach, father, author and experienced leader in the business community, I've seen the good and bad side of youth sports and can speak openly about cases where children's lives have truly been enhanced by sports. I've also seen the dark side of sports and have watched those who have ended up quitting because of the various pressures that became too overwhelming. I combine my personal experience with some of the latest research on human behavior to better understand what drives parents, coaches and children to behave the way that they do. My strategies will help you to make more informed decisions and be intentional in setting your children up for positive experiences in youth sports.

I strive to help parents to be honest in identifying their own motivations for enrolling their kids in youth sports and then create a purpose and intentional plan to ensure that their children's lives will be enriched through a lifetime worth of benefits acquired through participation.

Whether you have children who have not yet participated in sports or your children currently play sports and love them, you can create purpose and meaning behind your parenting approach and use the experiences as a means to have healthier and happier children.

The following chapters will take you through the youth sports experience from various angles and help you to better understand the good, bad and the ugly. My hope/intention, with this book, is to lead you on a path to self-discover the right plan to ensure your children experience all of the positives and minimize the negatives in youth sports.

Enjoy

1

How Pure Are Our Intentions?

The first question parents need to ask ourselves is what are the true motives for enrolling our children in sports for the first time? This may be the most important question to ask ourselves and be able to answer as honestly as possible. If our intentions are pure, it is important to revisit those motives on an annual basis as kids get older and we see the level of play start to get more competitive. I doubt when most parents enroll their child in youth sports for the first time at three, four or five years old, and they observe the organized chaos that is typical at that age, they think they'll ever get to the point of pressuring, cajoling or screaming at their child. Unfortunately in too many cases, this is the point many parents reach and this is usually the time when kids stop having fun playing sports.

If the real answer to this question has to do more with the parents than the benefits the child will receive, then one might as well not even enroll their kids to play sports in the first place. Imagine the dad who was an all-state quarterback who had tremendous success, but was too small to get any looks by college recruiters. Or how about the mom or dad who was an elite high school athlete who had a devastating injury that prematurely ended his or her dream of becoming a professional athlete? Or how about the parent who got cut from the basketball team and whose sense of self-worth was directly tied to not making the team? All of the cool kids played on the varsity team and he or she didn't feel a part of the "in crowd" and some of those memories continue to haunt them, even today.

Too often we see parents who want to live vicariously through their children and at a deep subconscious level, they strive to make up for their own past or current inadequacies. They look to have their own self esteem boosted through the praise, recognition or accolades their child receives and measure their social status as a parent against these accomplishments. They use their child's status in youth sports as a measuring stick for their own effectiveness as parents.

That same dad I mentioned earlier, who was an all-state quarterback, is determined to have his son Johnny play football and he's going to be a quarterback. He then starts him down the path with early instruction, specialization and gives his son every possible tool to be successful. If somewhere along the line Johnny is passionate about football, and he wants to spend all of his waking time becoming a great football player, then I'd say that dad should continue to "fan that flame" and support that passion. However, if along the way Johnny only plays football because that's what his dad wants him to do, then the fun will disappear, Johnny may quit or worse, he may resent his dad for years to come.

In my experience coaching youth sports, I've seen numerous instances where dads coach their son or daughter's team just so they feel as though they can better control their kid's opportunities and overall experience while playing the sport. This is where youth sports get the reputation of being political because coaches like this tend to favor their kids by granting them more playing time, play them at the most popular positions or make sure their son or daughter makes the all-star teams.

Once some parents start shelling out money on private coaches, instruction, travel teams or "elite teams" they sometimes start to develop a mindset that they want to get a return on their investment. Visions of college scholarships or the possibility of a professional career start to surface. Deep down I think most parents know the odds are not good for their child to play professional sports, but as their child starts to develop and become more competitive they might lose sight of just how much the odds are stacked against them to earn a college scholarship, let alone play sports professionally.

Some overly optimistic parents might point to the Gronkowski family whose son Rob is a star for the New England Patriots. Within the last few years, Rob had two other brothers playing in the NFL at the same time for a total of three siblings playing professional football at the same time. This is quite the anomaly as ESPN.com has calculated the odds of something like this happening being somewhere in the neighborhood of one in thirty-one million.

A recent poll from NPR, the Robert Wood Johnson Foundation and the Harvard T.H. Chan School of Public Health, indicates 26 percent of U.S. parents whose children in high school play sports hope their child will become a professional athlete one day. The same study states that for families with household incomes of less than $50,000 annually, the number is closer to 39 percent.

This represents a big disconnect between what the real odds are versus the perceived odds are that a child might have the potential to make it to the professional ranks. With the level of income that today's professional athletes are making, overambitious parents look at their children as their "meal ticket" to earning big money. This unrealistic attitude can be the root of misguided motives and behaviors that can cause parents to behave in negative ways.

There is a larger contingency of parents who might think the odds are stacked against their kids to play professionally but that a college scholarship would be a realistic return on their investment. There is a lot of data out there but one of the surveys I found suggests even that thought is a "pipe dream". A 2012 survey in CBS Moneywatch reported staggering information about the odds of earning a college scholarship. Amongst their findings:

- Only about 2 percent of high school athletes win sports scholarships every year at NCAA colleges and universities and for those who do earn a scholarship, the average value is less than $11,000.
- There are only six sports where all of the scholarships are full rides. These sports include football, men's and women's basketball, women's gymnastics, volleyball and tennis.
- Beyond the afore-mentioned sports, all other sports are considered "equivalency" sports. NCAA rules dictate how much money a program such as lacrosse or track, can spend on scholarships. (O'Shaughnessy, 2012)[1].

Therefore, for parents whose true motivation is to earn a return on their investment for the money they've poured into their children's athletic careers, many of them will be sorely disappointed when those dreams are not fulfilled. These types of aspirations typically yield the type of behavior that's overbearing and in many instances causes the child to lose the joy for the sport and ultimately quit.

The paradox is those who do end up making it to the college or professional levels typically have an undying love for the sport they play and are self-motivated to work and improve on their game, which perpetuates even greater performance. Often times the behaviors of overbearing or over involved parents has the opposite effect on their children pushing their child to want to quit or just go through the motions to appease mom and dad instead of continuing to play because they are passionate about the sport.

Aside from the financial burden and extensive time commitment travel sports place on the parents, the children see the increased burden as well. Considering all of the travel, practice, extended seasons, regional and all-star tournaments, that come along with these commitments, kids find themselves playing for much of the year without a break. Prior to the increase in popularity of travel sports, the most popular youth sports had much more defined seasons. We'd see baseball in the spring and summer, football and soccer in the fall and basketball in the winter.

It is much harder for kids to play multiple sports when a travel team season takes up a good portion of a child's time during the course of the year. Without being able to participate in different sports, kids may miss the benefits that come with exposure to cross-functional movements, different sets of rules and might miss out on a sport they are truly passionate about.

Some parents may argue when they grew up they were constantly playing pick-up sports year round and didn't just solely play organized sports. Therefore parents may have been playing sports year round in a less organized fashion, but year round nonetheless. This is similar to today's year- round travel team participants. There may be some truth to this but playing "pick-up" sports that are self-governed, lack structure, and are free from the scrutiny and judgment of adults, don't place children under the same microscope that can come along with year-round participation in organized sports.

It's disappointing to learn organizations like Little League, which has been around since 1939 and whose precepts are built upon leadership, character, courage and loyalty, have reported declining participation numbers in recent years. Some of this can be attributed to the increasing popularity of travel teams. The allure, prestige and promises that parents hear from travel team coaches, suggesting their child will play against better competition and will have more overall exposure, is tempting enough for many to invest their time and money to ensure they are giving their child the best possible chance to be successful.

I still have vivid memories of participating in Little League baseball as a child and I learned a lot of valuable lessons from that experience. The foundation of Little League prioritizes teaching life lessons to our children that will serve them for their whole lives, all the while competing locally with good competition. Additionally, the more traditional season that is typical of Little League has a true end and frees children up to pursue other passions or interest and create balance in their lives.

The fact that we have more access to information today than ever before including various forms of social media, the Internet, YouTube, this may feed into parents' unreasonable beliefs their child is destined to be a star because they've seen many examples of young phenoms having large amounts of success at a young age. In today's environment, anyone can look up old episodes on YouTube that show two-year-old Eldrick "Tiger" Woods hitting golf balls on the Mike Douglass show in the late 1970's. There are many other videos out there highlighting young prodigies accomplishing amazing things at a very early age in their respective sport. For some parents, this may feed into the notion that starting kids earlier is better and this early start gives their child a big advantage over others who may have started sports at a slightly older age.

Many of the misguided motives we've discussed cause parents to develop a "win at all cost" mentality because they are so serious about their kids keeping pace with others and not falling behind. When multiple parents on a team or in a league have this type of thought process, pressures are not just felt by the children playing the youth sports. Coaches, referees and even other parents are sometimes on the receiving end of very poor behavior because these unrealistic expectations can bring out the worst in people.

Imagine how the overbearing parent, who has poured thousands of dollars into the best instruction and equipment for their child, acts if their child's coach gives minimal playing time, places them in the "wrong" position or happens to bat them in a spot in the batting order that is reserved for lesser players. The disillusioned parent may look at this coach as a barrier to their child's success. How is my son or daughter going to make the high school team or travel team and ultimately earn a scholarship if the coach refuses to play them? Or I'm certain that my son is better than the kid who is the starting quarterback or starting shortstop! Or it's not fair the coach plays his son over my son when my son is better. Unfortunately, I've seen some of these scenarios unfold before my very eyes during my years of participating and coaching.

Coaching youth sports can be a very rewarding experience but more often than not it can be a very thankless position. Most youth coaches don't make any money for their countless hours they invest into making sure the team they are coaching is successful. Most coaches, including myself, are working parents who have a primary job that provides a living for their family. Not only does coaching take up a lot of the parents' free time, but in some cases the extra responsibilities might take away from the primary job because coaches decided to slip out of work to arrive early for games or stay up late to organize practices. In many cases, league administrators are desperate to find enough coaches so dedicated parents begrudgingly volunteer to coach because no one else will do it and they want the kids to have a good experience.

There are some instances where coaches may have poor intentions in volunteering to coach. They know by coaching they most likely will have an ability to control their son or daughter's playing time and not take the chance that another coach might not give them as much playing time as they'd like. More often than not, volunteer coaches have pure intentions and want to be as objective as possible. Actually, for many conscientious coaches, their involvement can "backfire" for their own child. I've known coaches that are so concerned with whether or not they're perceived as being fair, that they are extra hard on their own child. They make sure every child gets a chance to play or play different positions when maybe their own child is actually one of the best players on the team.

Referees are in a similar situation when it comes to volunteering their time and they typically make very little money to referee or umpire games. When I was in high school, I had some experience umpiring youth baseball games. I did make a little bit of money but I also did it to spend more time around one of the sports I truly enjoyed. You might be shocked to see some of what I saw and heard. Considering some of the reactions of the parents, to calls they felt that I made incorrectly, you'd think the kids were playing in Game 7 of the World Series! The profanity and name calling adults would place upon a high school kid was quite eye-opening. I'm not saying I was the best umpire out there but I also would never expect to be treated that way by otherwise respectable members of society.

My experience illustrates just how much self-imposed pressure some parents can place on themselves, their kids, coaches and referees and can cause behavior that is less than desirable. I don't believe many of the primary culprits of unruly behavior even realize they act this way. I would almost recommend most sporting leagues have a parents-only meeting prior to the start of the season to provide firm expectations and explain appropriate behavior. It might also be impactful to show a brief video of real footage that highlights parents acting in a manner that is hard to believe. At the end of the meeting every parent could be required to sign a "contract" which ultimately shows that they are agreeing to the code of conduct of acceptable parental behavior that has been laid out for them.

Mike Matheny, who is the current coach for the St. Louis Cardinals, wrote a book called "The Matheny Manifesto," an in-depth look at what he felt the role that parents should play in their children's youth sporting experience. Matheny was asked to coach his son's youth baseball team back in 2008 and he wrote a long letter to the parents. The letter began…"Dear Fellow Parents: I've always said I would coach only a team of orphans. Why?

Because the biggest problem in youth sports is the parents" (Connection, 2015)i . This letter was the foundation for the book that he ended up writing. Ultimately, he essentially tried to experiment and take the parents out of the equation as much as possible. His unique approach to coaching brought with it some interesting rules such as parental silence, focus on developing the person first before the athlete and encouraging coaches to communicate what they stand for rather than getting sucked into what others wanted.

A lot of what's wrong with youth sports can be attributed to the misguided intentions or motives of parents as they continue with their children down the path of their youth sports careers. Throughout the rest of this book we will discuss the great benefits of youth sports participation and why I am so passionate about using sports as a vehicle to guide, teach, coach and mentor our children. Sports give us an opportunity to mold youth into contributing members of society and ultimately successful adults.

In order for our children to experience all of the great benefits through youth sports participation, it is important that parents create a clear vision for how they would like to see participation shape the lives of their children. While creating any vision or establishing a purpose, it is important to begin with the end in mind. Visualize your child at his or her first communion, high school graduation, college graduation, first job, wedding and birth of a child. How do you envision your child? The type of people we visualize our children as can serve as our "guiding light" that will help to shape our actions and behaviors on a daily, weekly, monthly and yearly basis.

If our focus and attention remains fixed on this very clear vision then we will all be able to keep better perspective along our journey. Getting cut from a team, striking out, losing the big game and "riding the bench" are all things that will happen to kids at some point or another in our lives. These are the types of scenarios that could potentially create negative parental behavior. If we see those events as "teachable moments" and use them as metaphors to teach kids about overcoming adversity throughout their lives, we can continually reinforce the type of behavior that builds strong character in our children.[2]

Establishing a clear vision is important, but you would be remiss if your vision did not include keeping the fun in the sports for your child. As you're creating a vision for your children's sports experiences, pay attention to see whether or not your children have big smiles on their faces during this journey. Can you see them laughing and joking with their friends? Prioritizing "the fun factor" is probably one of the most important things we can focus on during our children's time participating in youth sports. Participation is crucial and the more years that our kids continue to play sports, the longer they can be exposed to these valuable lessons.

When the fun disappears, so does participation. That's the point where we see kids start to quit, go through the motions or lose their passion. As discussed, this can happen because of the undue pressures placed on the kids from the parents. But if the parents are focused on keeping the kids smiling, laughing and having fun, then the kids' actions will align with this vision and are more likely to want to keep playing. So take the time to plot out all of the great life lessons and benefits you plan on exposing your children to during their time in youth sports and remember to keep the priority on the kids having fun. If you do this and revisit your vision regularly, your kids will look back upon their time playing sports with great fondness and will want to someday pass down the same experiences to their children.

2

Health Benefits of Youth Sports

Think about the time in a child's life when he or she transitions from crawling to walking. The child becomes more efficient while walking and eventually he or she seems to be in the happiest state when running, falling, jumping, chasing and being chased all while smiling, giggling and laughing.

While picturing this, you might even break into a smile while visualizing kids taking part in those types of activities. Almost all people, whether they grow up to be athletic or not, seem to find enjoyment and a general state of happiness at the earliest ages, while participating in even the most basic forms of exercise.

With this in mind, why is it we hear so much about childhood obesity increasing at alarming rates? Generally speaking, kids today are far less active when compared to children from previous generations. According to a 2014 National Health and Examination Survey, "roughly 16 percent of children and adolescents between the ages of 6-19 years are considered to be overweight" (Vincent Ianelli, 2014). Some of the reasons that were given were poor nutrition, lack of physical activity, genetics and lack of sleep.

One could argue a person's genetic predispositions would be relative to previous generations and could be characterized as remaining static. As far as nutrition is concerned, it seems reasonable to draw a conclusion that today's larger portions combined with more processed food options, might be leading to an increase in children who are overweight. Lack of sleep might be relative to previous generations however, there are studies indicating increased exposure to screen time or technology (i.e. television, iPads, smart phones, computers), especially close to bed time, can make it more difficult for people to fall asleep. For our purposes, we'll look more closely at how a lack of physical activity can lead to overweight or obese children who develop habits that can carry into adulthood.

We live in an exciting world today where many enjoy the benefits and convenience from technology. Think about all the gadgets and toys that are prevalent in today's society, including smartphones, laptops, iPads, smart watches, interactive TV's, Siri, Bluetooth, video games, hands free devices. I'll now challenge you to be observant the next time you're out in a public place and you see parents out with their young children. I think it's safe to say you'll see many iPads, iPhones, computers, electronic toys in the hands of many children. Many times these devices are used as mechanisms to control kids' behavior while in public.

An argument can be made that kids today are becoming more tech savvy at earlier ages than ever before. One positive is this may help kids adapt to future classroom settings, as it becomes more the norm for these types of devices to be used as supplements or aids to the learning processes in classrooms. It's common for kids to spend countless hours at home with their heads buried in these gadgets. Many times parents know if they're doing things around the house their children will be content playing with these "toys" for long stretches of time. I can attest that as much as I am aware of it and want to control the amount of "screen time" my own kids get that it is sometimes easy to succumb to the convenience of allowing our children play with these devices.

If you watch children's behavior, while using a variety of these different devices, it's easy to see how these gadgets can become so addictive. It's as if they're drawn to a far-away place or a trance-like state while immersed in this technology and time seems to slip away. It can get to the point the gadget of choice becomes the primary toy, which often leads to more time indoors. Many have heard people who grew up in previous generations comment on how they spent much of their time outdoors playing in the neighborhood and had to be "dragged" back inside when it was dinner time. I was born in the mid- 1970s and have vivid memories from my childhood of summers where I spent a majority of my time playing outside from sunrise to sundown. When school was back in session, I'd finish my homework as soon as possible so that I could go outside and play.

I'm sure there are plenty of children who still enjoy playing outside and are very active, but generally speaking, it does seem the more complex technology gets, the less active kids become. It takes intentional parenting to strive to simplify things for our kids today and steer them towards physical activity and work to minimize the use of technology or "screen time" during the early years.

The National Football League, which is by far the most popular professional sports league in the United States, launched a program called "NFL Play 60" back in 2007. The NFL has been consistent in their messaging ever since. The program encourages children to be active for at least sixty minutes per day. The NFL has aired many commercials and various forms of advertising ever since they launched the program to share their message of encouraging children to get outside and play for at least an hour per day.

The NFL published some statistics they updated in July of 2012 on NFL.com, in support of their Play 60 initiative, that included the following:

• The current generation is projected to be the first not to live longer than its parents.
• One third of children in America are obese or are at risk for obesity.
• Ninety-two percent of Americans believe childhood obesity is a serious national problem.
• Only eight percent of elementary schools provide daily physical education

The last point highlights only a small percentage of elementary schools still provide daily physical education by still offering gym class and recess. Gym class and recess were both staples in school when I was growing up and in previous generations. Some schools may have done away with different forms of physical education in an effort to save money given dwindling budgets. Whatever the reason, kids are not getting as much of an opportunity to participate in physical activity during school hours.

There are studies that suggest regular activity can have a positive effect on brain development and learning. A 2010 study conducted at the University of Illinois at Urbana-Champaign concluded "fit children tend to have a bigger hippocampus and perform better on a test of memory than their less fit peers." In the study, magnetic resonance imaging (MRI's) were used to study the brain activity of kids who could be considered fit versus those who were not, and the results of the study helped researchers conclude physical activity and fitness can have a positive impact on children's developing brains.

Participation in youth sports is a great way to ensure our kids are getting consistent exercise, considering kids are getting fewer opportunities to be active during school hours. When kids are playing sports they usually have multiple practices per week in which they are engaging in physical activity and exercise. Combine that with games and unstructured play outside, to supplement the exercise that kids can get in more organized sports, and that leads to a winning combination. Children who really enjoy playing sports may want to stay in shape or train for the sports they play, even outside of the season and this further promotes high fitness levels.

As many kids grow up, it can be a process for them to get to the point they're comfortable in their own skin. Participation in sports is a great way to improve a child's confidence levels. Participation in a team or other types of groups can help give children a sense of belonging and pride. I hear a lot of stories today about childhood bullying and how many schools are trying to put bullying prevention programs in place. Bullying has always been a reality, but the perception might be that it occurs at a greater frequency today since news and information is able to be shared so much easier through social media and the internet.

Kids that get bullied can sometimes feel alone and they have nowhere to turn. I have a story that is personal to me because I found out what a close family friend's child was going through. This couple's twelve year old daughter (we'll call her Jenna) started to act very differently at home. Jenna normally shared everything with her parents about school, friends and activities. The parents noticed their daughter's behavior had changed. She would go to her room and spend a lot of time behind closed doors. Jenna was sleeping more than normal and she also seemed very irritable and short with her parents. She wasn't confiding nearly as much in her parents as they were used to and her overall behavior was noticeably different.

One day the doorbell rang and Jenna's mom opened the door to find one of Jenna's classmates and her mother at the door. The mother told Jenna's mom they had seen hateful messages written about Jenna by other kids through their daughter's Instagram social media account. She went on to describe some of the hurtful messages that were written about Jenna including "I hope you die", "you're worthless", "you're ugly," and other messages that can crush any child's self-esteem. Thank goodness Jenna's parents found out about it when they did and were able to intervene. They were able to address it through the school and the parents of the children who were writing the messages.

Sadly, not all of these types of stories have happy endings. Childhood suicide, as a result of bullying, happens far more often than it should. Childhood can be tough because kids can be very vulnerable and insecure during some of the awkward stages they'll experience throughout childhood and into adolescence. Negative experiences of being bullied or picked on can have lasting effects on a person throughout his or her life. Participation in sports can help to build up confidence levels to combat some of the difficulties that kids naturally go through. The activity or exercise that comes along with playing sports allows our brains to release endorphins which are "feel good" chemicals that enhance our moods. This type of regular activity helps to counteract feelings of depression of any type.

The exercise that comes along with playing youth sports not only helps to promote childhood fitness and combat obesity, it also helps to establish groundwork that will hopefully lead to a lifetime love of exercise. Kids that get accustomed to working out and training for their current sport, or train on their own for an upcoming sport, will learn to crave all of the things that make us feel good about exercising. These include increased strength, stronger bones and growth, to name a few. Years of exercising will establish a foundation that will hopefully promote less sedentary lifestyles as kids grow into adulthood.

A current phenomenon gaining tremendous popularity over the last five years is CrossFit. CrossFit is known as the "sport of exercise" where people compete in various workouts and different forms of Olympic weight training combined with cardiovascular exercise. CrossFit's annual showcase which is known as the CrossFit games is now nationally televised and has allowed people like multiple time winner, Rich Froning, to emerge as a celebrities. I personally joined a CrossFit gym close to where I work for about a year and I thoroughly enjoyed the experience. Crossfit "boxes" or gyms do a great job of establishing a sense of community or belonging and also of tapping into the competitive spirit of each individual. When someone starts out in CrossFit, he or she might feel overwhelmed because the movements don't come naturally. Each person establishes their own baseline and over time ends up competing with his or herself in the pursuit of achieving a new "personal best." More and more CrossFit gyms have started to offer CrossFit for Kids which in many cases is offered to children ages four and up. Kids this age learn to do different types of bodyweight exercise that are safe and appropriate for their age. I've observed some of the classes and it's amazing how much kids seem to smile and enjoy themselves while participating in strenuous exercise.

As I watched kids in the CrossFit classes, I wished I would have been exposed to this type of training when I was playing sports in my childhood because these types of workouts would help to prepare you for just about any sport. The beauty of CrossFit is even if your child does not play sports at all, he or she can start to develop a passion for exercising, which will serve them well for years to come.

CrossFit memberships cost money. This can be a barrier for budget-conscious parents who might not have the resources to enroll their kids in programs such as CrossFit or sports leagues. Creative parents can find low-cost or no-cost ways for their kids to get more exercise. For example, there are a lot of apps for smartphones and free websites out there that offer different workouts for people to try. Performing some of these exercises with your kids might prompt them to want to exercise and they will also benefit by spending time with their mom or dad.

Organized sports and exercise are a great option but there seems to be far less unstructured play that occurs today versus that in previous generations. If you live in good neighborhoods with a lot of children, then there might be opportunity to allow your kids to play out in your neighborhood with other kids. Kids might not even play sports, but play games such as hide and seek or capture the flag that involves a lot of running around. Depending on where you live, active neighborhoods might be less prevalent in today's society but being intentional about exposing your kids to physical activity might mean taking them to the park or other types of common areas where they are free to run around and play.

As kids get older and want to continue playing sports, they'll often start to get more serious about training on their own for their sport. A side benefit of this is that is natural to want to eat healthier when training so that any gains that they see from training can be maximized. Kids who are trying to be the best they can be often learn to create better eating habits or think of eating more as a way of fueling their body. This again can help to build good habits or a strong foundation as they get older and become adults where they might be more conscious of what they put in their body. Obesity is not just a childhood epidemic, but appears to be on the rise in adults as well, along with heart disease and various other forms of illness. Exposing our children to good eating habits during their youth can help to combat these concerns. If participation in youth sports helps to solidify this message then ultimately, we will all be in better health!

Some sports can be played well past high school and enjoyed for a lifetime. Sports like tennis, golf, racquetball, swimming, running are just some examples that people can learn to enjoy and still participate in throughout their lives. The beauty of these types of sports is they are fun and when we participate in them we can stay fit without the monotony that traditional gym equipment can sometimes bring. I enjoy playing golf as I approach the age of 40 and know that when I walk during a round of golf that I'll walk the equivalent of approximately five miles.

Encouraging children to exercise at a young age, and establish good physical habits, helps them to value exercise and start down the path to living healthy and happy lives. Parents need to develop an intentional strategy to combat some of today's challenges that naturally lead to less activity and exercise. Participation in youth sports is one of the best ways I can think of to condition our kids to acquire healthy habits that can yield longstanding benefits for the rest of their lives. This is hard to achieve if our kids don't want to participate and this is something we'll tackle as we move forward in this book.

3

Participation is the name of the game

In the beginning of the book, I've discussed some of the great benefits children can experience while playing youth sports. I will continue to highlight these benefits throughout this book. For children to benefit from youth sports, the first simple step is participation. If our kids choose not to participate in sports, or they prematurely drop out, then they will miss out on the "teachable moments" that happen on the journey while playing youth sports. Parents will also lose the opportunity to use youth sports as a vehicle to shape our kids in a positive way through these experiences.

According to the University of Notre Dame's Center for Ethical Education, research shows kids play sports for the following reasons:

- To have fun (always the #1 reason!)
- To do something I am good at
- To improve my skills
- To get exercise and stay in shape
- To be a part of a team
- The excitement of competition

The reasons mentioned above are examples of pure intentions of why kids will try a sport for the first time. These reasons motivate kids to participate and try a sport they might be curious about. What happens, along the way that may cause kids to quit participating in youth sports? This topic will be the main focus of this chapter.

I've seen many different surveys reporting figures of the percentage of children that drop out of youth sports at a young age. An average of what I've seen suggests roughly 70% of kids drop out of organized athletics by age thirteen. Some reasons given are financial and time constraints, but most kids stop playing when they no longer find participation is sports to be fun. Parents, coaches and league organizers play very different roles in youth sports and also have the highest level of influence on the kids who are participating. These critical roles can serve as catalysts for change and can either make or break the youth sports experience.

Based on my experience and the above-mentioned research, I've concluded some level of participation in sports is better than none at all. With this in mind, I will tackle an issue that seems to be a lightning rod for controversy. The notion that "everyone gets a trophy" seems to be controversial, as I've heard people passionately support both sides of the argument. As a lifelong fan and avid supporter of the Pittsburgh Steelers, I paid particular attention to a headline that involved a well-known Steelers player, James Harrison, who shared his view on the topic. Given his status as a professional athlete, his opinion was "heard" by a large number of people through national sports outlets and his large following on different social media platforms. I follow some of Harrison's posts, and overall, admire him for his tremendous work ethic and devotion as a dad to his two sons.

On his social media accounts, Harrison posted a picture of two trophies that his six and eight- year- old sons were each given just for being "participants" in some sort of sport. Harrison posted the following comments on his various social media accounts:

"I came home to find out that my boys received two trophies for nothing, participation trophies! While I am very proud of my boys for everything they do and will encourage them till the day I die, these trophies will be given back until they EARN a real trophy. I'm sorry I'm not sorry for believing that everything in life should be earned and I'm not about to raise two boys to be men by making them believe that they are entitled to something just because they tried their best…because sometimes your best is not enough, and that should drive you to want to do better…not cry and whine until somebody give you something to shut you up and keep you happy.

#harrisonfamilyvalues"

After James Harrison posted these comments, his views gained national exposure on ESPN and various other sports talk radio shows. Most callers sided with Harrison's take and many stated trophies should be earned and we shouldn't be teaching kids that everyone gets a trophy. I, for one, used to support this side of the argument and believed the notion that "everyone gets a trophy" may be one reason for a generation of kids who feel entitled to receive benefit or praise, even if it hasn't necessarily been earned.

As someone who has 15 of my 17 years in the workforce, in different managerial or leadership positions, I began to perceive younger generations seemed to possess an attitude of entitlement. I also began to generalize younger generations tend to look for more immediate gratification. With this type of approach, there doesn't seem to be much room for patience for youth to wait for good things, like promotions or other types of achievements, to happen. Some of my opinions may have originally shaped my belief that coddling today's kids, or giving them rewards for just showing up, will lead to more kids feeling a sense of entitlement.

My position on this debate has changed and I now can see the other side of the argument. Throughout my experience of coaching youth sports, and now seeing my own son start to participate in sports, I believe participation in general is THE most important thing! At the end of the season, if certain leagues or organizations want to reward kids for participating and "everyone gets a trophy," then so be it.

I am more open-minded to different approaches, as more and more evidence paints the picture of just how many kids are prematurely dropping out of sports and participating in sports at a lower rate than in previous generations. I am most passionate about the concept that parents and coaches need to do whatever they can to make sports fun so kids participate fully and ultimately want to keep on playing. It's not until they are having fun, and come back year after year, that kids will be exposed to and benefit from the values and lessons that come along with being part of a team.

As I mentioned earlier, overzealous parents with misguided motives often enroll their kids in one sport or multiple sports that require attending a game or practice nearly every night of the week. Parents who have more than one child participating in sports at the same time, may be trying to manage such complex schedules they might have trouble deciphering if they're coming or going. It's important for parents to be careful and selective in choosing what league to play in or whether or not to have kids playing in more than one sport at a time. The moment it starts to feel like more of a job, kids may start to dread going to practice and games. If this happens, then kids may want to focus additional time and effort in other areas of interest. It's important to research a league and the coach ahead of time to gain a good understanding of what level of commitment is expected for the kids and the parents. Again, the number one priority is to have fun, and it's hard to have fun when participation in a sport starts to feel like a chore.

I also mentioned earlier in the book, about parents who may have misguided motives for enrolling their kids in sports in the first place. The profiles of the parents who live vicariously through their children's successes or failures in youth sports tend to behave in a manner that suffocates their kids. If children feel constantly berated, micromanaged forced to practice or get yelled at consistently, it will not be a good experience. This approach ultimately works against the goal of encouraging participation, which is contradictory to the goal of exposing children to the great lessons that can be learned through sports. Even if children don't drop out of sports because they feel their parents are forcing them to play, they might come to resent the sport and even worse, resent their parents.

In the book, "the Matheny Manifesto," Mike Matheny, shared "parents were the biggest problem in youth sports." Matheny, who is the manager for the St. Louis Cardinals, was approached about coaching his son's youth baseball team, and he put a lot of thought into the rules and principles he would put into place in the form of a letter he wrote to the parents. Once he laid out these expectations, the parents could then decide if they would agree to the terms if he were to coach the team. The letter ultimately ended up becoming famously referred to as the "Matheny Manifesto" and was the basis for his book. There were a number of comments on behaviors addressed in the letter, but one that stood out to me was parents had to remain silent during the games. I believe the parents were allowed to clap and that was about it! The argument is kids already seek their parents' approval in general, and even if parents are yelling words of encouragement, it still takes kids' attention away from the game and their coaches.

It is probable parents will face a time when their child will say they want to quit their sport. I think it's reasonable to have the child finish out the season in hopes of instilling the lesson that it's important to finish what we start. If a child does not want to play the next season, then it's probably best not to force them. As disappointing as it may be, that our child wants to quit "our favorite sport," giving them a break might help the child come to realize they miss it and ultimately want to start playing again.

This brings me to an interesting concept of extrinsic vs. intrinsic motivation and how each may affect the actions and behaviors of not just kids, but people in general. Dr. John Tauer is the professor of psychology at the University of St. Thomas. A lot of his research focuses on the factors leading to intrinsic motivation in people. What I think is unique about Dr. Tauer is as a psychology professor with a Ph.D., he already has a good understanding of human behavior and he is also a college basketball coach at the same university where he teaches. What better laboratory to test his findings and concepts, while coaching students who come together and accomplish a common goal on the basketball court.

As a leader in a business setting, where I'm responsible for the productivity or output of over 100 people, I've read a lot about the concepts of intrinsic and extrinsic motivation. I'm open to learning new ways to better motivate a large workforce to maximize their potential in to achieve their business objectives. Dr. John Tauer wrote a book called "Why Less is More for WOSPs (Well-Intentioned, Overinvolved Sports Parents): How to be the Best Sports Parent you can Be". In his book he combines his expertise in the study of psychology and human behavior with his own examples as a coach and shares concrete examples that illustrate this point. I think Dr. Tauer does a great job simplifying the notion of intrinsic motivation into a few basic things that must be present for individuals to be motivated.

My interpretation of intrinsic motivation is to have a strong desire from within to do something that will bring inner pleasure by participating in a certain activity. Extrinsic motivation is more dependent upon rewards, incentives, money etc. to provoke someone into performing. To test what we may be intrinsically motivated to do, we can think about what we want to do with a day off of work, where no one is dictating our actions. The things we might choose to do in that context are most likely the things we're more intrinsically motivated to do. In Dr. Tauer's book, he boiled it down to three factors that if present, can lead to intrinsic motivation in people. He cited "autonomy," "relatedness" and "competency" as the three factors that lead people to want to participate in an activity by their own choice. If parents think of this as a "three legged stool," where if all three factors are present, there is a much greater chance their children will want to participate in youth sports.

"Autonomy" has to do with having the freedom to choose what activities to participate in without outside influence from others. Therefore, overbearing parents who want to control every aspect of a child's schedule will find that this type of behavior counter to what would encourage the child to play the sport on their own. Autonomy is the key to participation. If children continue to play a sport on their own, and not because they feel forced to, this "choice" will increase their enjoyment and fun, make it feel less like a chore and ultimately keep kids coming back year after year.

For our purposes, "relatedness" has to do with the relationships developed between teammates, coaches and others affiliated with youth sports. Many of us can attest when our kids started playing sports; a favorite moment might be going for ice cream with their friends after the game. Other moments of connection for kids might be making friends with the other kids on their team, which encourages them to keep coming back. In addition, relatedness might also look like a great coach who has a profound impact on a child and his or her ability to relate. The coach's relationship with that child might be the driving force for making he or she want to continue to play.

"Competency" can help motivate children to want to play a sport if they feel confident in their skills in that sport. If a child starts playing baseball and doesn't know how to throw, catch, hit, or feel they are far below the skill level of most of their teammates, that child may not give baseball much of a chance. Prior to enrolling kids in a sport for the first time, parents can work to develop skills so their child will feel somewhat competent in that sport or activity when they show up on day one. This should help the child feel confident enough so he or she can truly enjoy the experience.

To ensure all three of the above-mentioned motivators are present for my children and others I coach, my personal strategy is to work on the elements in a certain order. With my kids, I focus on competency first and try to accomplish this by making games out of drills designed to develop skills related to the specific sport. I get as creative as possible when making up games designed to improve my son's skill level, yet still make it fun so we continue to make progress. I've done this with any sport I've considered enrolling him in, so he goes into his first practice with at least a baseline understanding of what his coach will be asking him to do. He certainly does not need to have the best skills compared to his teammates, but showing up with some confidence makes it less likely that he will feel overwhelmed. If he's not worried about his skills being inadequate, compared to the other kids, then he is much more likely to dive in, have fun and make some friends!

Next, I cultivate an environment in which my son builds relationships with other teammates and his coaches. Simple things like encouraging him to root for other kids when it's their turn or encouraging him to say goodbye to his teammates before we leave. Giving high fives when they do something well, keeping their spirits up if they make a mistake, and encouraging him to listen to his coach and other others all add up to positive interactions. Before you realize it, he has some friends, and others within the team environment, he wants to see on a daily and weekly basis. It can be these strong relationships that are what keeps my son to wanting to come back and keep participating.

When it comes to the order of the three motivators, I focus on autonomy last because if the other two factors are there, autonomy will usually fall in line. My experience tells me if kids feel confident enough in their skill level for the sport, and they're having fun with their teammates, you won't have to force them to participate. Quite the opposite, kids may actually be begging you to sign them up for the next season! When your kids actually enjoy the process and want to play, you're halfway to meeting your vision of having them experience all the benefits that sports have to offer.

Once you're to the point to where your children want to participate in sports, it's also important to pay attention to the coach who will be leading your very impressionable children. I mentioned this earlier, but it bears repeating most coaches volunteer their time to coach youth sports and it's often a thankless job. Most have a primary job and in many cases coaches are not compensated for the extra hours for their volunteer time. . This is very admirable and without them, our kids would not have the opportunity to play organized sports. With that being said, we still need to keep our eye out for the "bad apple" or the coach that is stuck in an "old-school" way of thinking. When many think of old school coaches, Vince Lombardi's famous quote, "Winning isn't everything, it's the only thing," often comes to mind.

It's unfortunate when youth coaches do not see the big picture and want to run their team in a "win at all costs" manner. This approach leads to playing only the best children and limiting the playing time of others. Yelling, screaming and long mundane practices might also be byproducts of this approach. This type of coach is fairly easy to spot and should be avoided, if possible. This is not to say your child's coach should never deliver hard messages or lessons, but there is a right and a wrong way to convey these messages in a way that is appropriate for young kids. When done in a constructive manner, these messages can leave a lasting imprint and can be very valuable for our children.

When I think of coaches who place a lot of emphasis on leading through relationship vs. leading in more of a transactional manner, I think of some of the following people: Mike Matheny, Brad Stevens, Tony Dungy, Pete Carroll and John Wooden. These individuals are high profile but they all have been very successful coaches who've made their mark in their respective sports by putting relationship first. None of these coaches have a reputation where they use harsh tones or profanity to control their players' behavior. This is contradictory to styles such as that of Bobby Knight and his reputation for screaming at players and officials. Another example is former Rutgers basketball coach, Mike Rice, who was caught on tape verbally abusing his players, which ultimately led to him losing his job. More recently Jim McElwain, who is the new head football coach for the University of Florida, was caught on camera screaming at the top of his lungs just a couple of inches from the face of one of his players who had just demonstrated a lack of sportsmanship. The anger this incident stirred up, quickly disappeared most likely because the team kept winning games.

Coaches often pick up tips from what they see on T.V. or coaches from their past and this can help form their coaching style. It's one thing for professional coaches to display questionable behavior if it's how they make their living and they are working with adults, but there is no excuse for parents to put up with one of their children's coaches acting in a manner which demeans kids because of a "win at all cost" mentality. Doing research ahead of time on the couch, whenever possible, might be time well spent if you can avoid a coach who does not demonstrate your values.

The right coach can have a huge impact on our children's lives. To this day, I can remember feedback I received from some of my youth sports coaches. I believe my experience growing up playing youth sports has led me to be more open to feedback as an adult and is the primary reason that I've adopted a personal growth mindset. A good coach can inspire a child to want to work harder and help create an intrinsically motivated child who wants to do things for the right reasons. Over the course of our children's lives, they will have good coaches and bad coaches and we can use our role as parents to draw parallels between these scenarios and ones they might encounter in their future. It's probably safe to say when our kids enter the workforce that the odds are they will have some good bosses and some really bad bosses.

If we see are kids are enjoying participating in youth sports, to the point where they proactively ask us if we can sign them up for the next sport, we can take comfort in knowing we're helping to create a positive sports experience for them. In fact, parents can use this strong desire to play or practice as leverage to encourage other types of important behaviors, such as finishing school work, doing chores and going to bed on time. I'm not advocating we threaten our kids, but if they don't complete other important tasks, parents can certainly limit play or practice time, which can very quickly lead to more desired behaviors from our kids.

Considering the topics discuss in this book, participation is arguably the most important. It is crucial to consider all of the factors that lead our kids to willingly participate in sports. If they stop having fun, or sports become too much of a job for them, they will become part of the growing trend of kids who are prematurely dropping out of sports at alarming rates. Challenge yourself to continually have your kids pass the most basic litmus test, which is the frequency you see them smiling and having fun! If fun is the name of the game, then you're on the right track.

4

Long lasting life lessons

The utilization of sports as a platform, that allows parents to create "teachable moments," might be the greatest benefit that youth sports can provide our kids. There is "gold" in these lessons, but we as parents need to be intentional about seeking them out and strive to communicate with our kids at a level they can understand so our kids can apply the lesson to their own life.

Teamwork

At some point in most people's lives they will be a part of a team, whether they play a sport a not. Being part of a team is inevitable, whether working in group setting in school, participating in various afterschool activities and eventually, in the workplace. Most teams have an objective or a mission and success or failure is dependent upon the ability of a group of individuals to come together to work towards achieving a common goal. In various leadership roles I have held in my professional life, I've experienced a lot of good teams and a lot of dysfunctional teams.

Unfortunately, it's uncommon for a group of people to come together and work harmoniously and put personal agendas aside in the spirit of doing what's right for the team to succeed. Most sports are team sports, which are reliant upon the principles of teamwork and the ultimate measuring stick is the scoreboard or the team's record. Even sports that are more individual in nature, like golf or tennis, are still in many cases tied to some sort of a team.

There are parallels that can be drawn from sports teams to teams in the workforce. There is typically a person who is designated as the leader, or coach, who is ultimately responsible for the performance of the group. Most often there is a defined mission or task the group is trying to accomplish. The most effective teams come together with an intangible energy that comes from everyone being on the same page. Roles start to become clear as teams develop, whether this happens by assignment or more informally.

It is also inevitable that our kids will be a part of some good teams and some bad teams along their journey. It's highly likely at some point our kids will have a bad coach just as they might have a bad boss someday. Hopefully, they'll play for some coaches who really make an impression on them and inspire them to put in the effort because they want to and not because they have to. Chances are, they'll always remember this coach and even some of the specific things the coach said to them. I can still remember how my 8th grade football coach inspired me through words and action and I wanted to be better because of him. Looking back on this is funny because I was a third string, undersized quarterback who didn't have a lot of impact on the team, yet the coach was still able to inspire me. Despite not being much of a contributor, I still look back upon that experience with great fondness.

Being a part of a team for the first time helps to teach people what it means to have responsibility and be accountable. I'm sure many of us have met our fair share of people in the workplace who we perceive to be selfish and how these types of people tend to alienate themselves. This type of behavior does not work well in a team setting and if a team is made up of too many of these types of people, the team more than likely won't be very successful. Conscientious team members regularly put others before themselves for the betterment of the group. Being accountable in a team setting means to be on time, follow the rules, be supportive to others and listen to authority figures. When our kids are a part of a team throughout their childhood, they will learn some of these valuable lessons. A parent can certainly accelerate this process by regularly pointing out scenarios they see occurring within the teams.

Parents can help your kids express what it is they like about his or her coach and what makes this coach effective. If they have a teammate who doesn't treat others well or doesn't listen to the coach, parents can talk with their kids about how those behaviors affect the entire team. There are many lessons to be highlighted if parents are aware, with eyes and ears open, and communicate what they are seeing. The sooner our kids learn to be great team members the better this will serve our kids throughout their lives and set them up for success in group settings.

Preparation

In Chapter 3, I mentioned autonomy as one of the primary components of intrinsic motivation. Let's assume our kids are exercising autonomy and are continuing in a sport because they want to play and not because they feel forced to participate. As our kids get more serious about their sport they may realize the level of commitment that comes along with that sport. Our kids may learn if they want to be successful, they'll have to work hard at the organized practices. Our kids may also start putting in time for that sport outside of the organized activities.

For example, when I was young, I remember getting ready for an upcoming season and the coaches handed out suggested workout plans to prepare us for the type of conditioning we'd be participating in when practice started. I would find myself working out on my own so I would be in the best possible shape when the season started. I wanted to keep up with the others and put my best foot forward. Many times, I remember getting together with other kids to have group workouts sessions to prepare for the upcoming season.

During the offseason in football, most teams usually have some form of organized conditioning and weight lifting programs. Even though these programs are outside of the actual season, this is where a lot of the physical improvements are made. I've seen many cases where kids have transformed themselves into bigger, stronger, faster athletes and come back the next season having made huge strides because of their efforts. To me, learning to prepare is a necessary skill to acquire, and is a common denominator, for people who experience success in their profession. The longer kids continue to play youth sports, and become more serious about it, they'll get better at learning how preparation correlates to better performance.

There is a certain level of discipline that is developed by those who work hard to prepare and are dedicated to working on their own. Discipline is also learned because of the structured nature of sports and kids learn how to take instruction from an authority figure and learn to follow the rules of their respective sport. Kids who put in the time to prepare for their sport will, more often than not, see their bodies transform and their skills improve, leading to increased confidence and self-esteem. This increased competency is part of the "three legged stool" of intrinsic motivation to go along with autonomy and relatedness. These elements together, will build confidence and should continue to fuel their desire to keep participating.

As parents, we can continue to be observant and reinforce these important lessons. We can point out how hard our child has been working and putting in the extra time in their sport. We can share with our kids how we've noticed they have improved in many areas. Ultimately, we can emphasize this sense of work ethic and preparation will serve our kids well the rest of their lives, as they strive for excellence in whatever they pursue.

Competition

Learning to compete is an important skill for kids to acquire to grow and reach their potential. Competition is part of the business world, where you may see multiple people competing for the same job, within an organization. There is also competition within an industry where companies are either thriving because they are highly effective in a competitive marketplace or going out of business. Competition is inherent in sports and those who are around sports for any lengths of time learn how to compete within their team and against other teams they are matched up against.

Competition is not always about comparing ourselves to someone else or some other thing. Often times a winner or a loser is declared, but there are other important elements to consider about competition. To me, competition is about learning to compete with ourselves and striving to be the best version of ourselves we can be. When people focus their time and energy on things they can control, such as striving to be their best self every day, they'll see continuous improvement and make progress towards maximizing their potential. As a hiring manager in a business setting, I am looking for employees who are driven to compete and feel comfortable in this type of environment.

When I was working out at a CrossFit gym, one thing I really liked about "the sport of fitness" element was that people kept track of their "PR" or personal record. By focusing on my personal best, it seemed to drive me to continually compete with myself and put in the work to achieve a new personal best. Myself and others take a lot of pride when they exceed what was their personal best the day or week before, and it can act as a good measuring stick to monitor improvement. Focusing on exceeding our own personal best is also within our control and through hard work; we can improve upon this regardless of outside influences. Those who think competing is always about comparing themselves to others, may feel overwhelmed at times. It's good to have a way to see how we stack up compared to others, but doing this too often can be counterproductive.

A better approach is having a "growth mindset." A growth mindset is one where a person believes he or she can always do slightly better at a certain skill, learn more or find more efficient ways of doing something. A "fixed mindset" is quite different, in that a person tends to label themselves as someone who can't be changed. Phrases such as "I'm not very artistic," "I'm not a good athlete" and "I'm not a good cook" are indicative of someone who has more of a fixed mindset.

Carol Dweck, a social psychologist at the University of Stanford, has done research and studied people who display characteristics of a growth mindset. These studies show there is a correlation between the most successful people, across different fields, and a growth mindset. Hard work, continuous improvement, reading and self-reflection tend to be elements that are synonymous with people who show this way of thinking. Dweck conducted studies with children showing participants were more motivated when given a mastery goal vs. a performance goal. With a mastery goal, the intent is to get better at something and if improvement or progress is shown there is a sense of fulfillment. When a performance goal is assigned and not met, people in general have a tendency to feel like a failure, because the goal has not been met.

This above-mentioned supports the notion that competing can be more about comparing oneself to previous personal bests, with an eye toward continuous improvement. Parents can support children in their development by reinforcing this mindset during their formative years.

Overcoming Adversity

The more life experience we gain, the more we learn life is full of adversity. How quickly people learn to adapt and overcome adversity is something that can help separate them from their peers. Overcoming adversity can be very difficult for children, whether it's as simple as losing their favorite toy or as complex as the death of a loved one. Even as adults, with years of experience under our belts, it can still be difficult to handle adversity when it rears it's ugly head; like the loss of a job, a home, a loved one, a child or a friend. Youth sports and sports in general, can give us healthy doses of adversity that help us parents in our quest to raise well-rounded children.

Imagine the following scenario: My son is up to bat in his baseball game in the last half inning of the game. His team is losing 3-2 but his team has loaded the bases and he is put in a unique position to win the game. The pitcher has thrown three straight balls, the count is 3-0, and he is one bad pitch away from drawing a walk, which would lead to the tying run. The next pitch is a called a strike that appeared to be low, so now the count is 3-1. The next pitch comes and my son swings and misses for strike two. Now it's a full count at 3-2 and with two outs the entire game rests on the next pitch. Here's the pitch….he swings at a ball that was thrown low, in the dirt, and misses for strike three! He's not only out but his team loses the game. A collective groan is heard by the crowd as they process the fact that the game is over.

As you can imagine, the ride home from the game is a tough one. My son was so upset he cried. He felt like he let his entire team down and failed in a moment when they needed him the most. If you compare this moment to the loss of a job or a death of a loved one, it pales in comparison, but to our sons or daughters this can feel like the worst thing in the world and their confidence may be completely shaken. These scenarios are fairly common for people who spend enough time playing sports. Facing adversity through losing the game, perceived failure in the game or getting cut from a team are all things that "come with the territory" in youth sports.

Even today, I have vivid memories of showing up for the last basketball tryouts for 7th grade basketball. My peers knew we would find out our fate at the end of that day's tryout, by seeing the final roster posted with cuts. I was an unfortunate one who got cut and I was devastated. I loved basketball and had practiced hard all summer in hopes I could make the team. This was difficult for me to process at that age and I was in a "funk" for a while after that. Eventually, I was able to shake it off and I decided to join the wrestling team. The silver lining of the story was I went on to wrestle for four years and I really enjoyed that experience and learned a lot.

Experiencing these types of scenarios in youth sports help to develop mental toughness at a young age. As parents, it is necessary for us to be there every step of the way, to not only support our broken hearted child when something doesn't go their way, but help them understand life is not always fair and we can all expect to experience painful things in our life. We can help our kids develop coping mechanisms, which will be useful as they continue to face adversity through sports and in life.

We can also teach our kids not to fear failure. Sometimes people become so consumed with being afraid to fail; it affects them in the current moment. Sports psychologists work with their clients on developing enough discipline to be in the present and focus all of their energy on the task at hand, instead of worrying about some way they messed up in the past or about how they might mess up in the future.

I used to struggle with this concept quite a bit while playing on the golf team in high school. If I was having a bad hole and was putting for a double-bogey, I might dwell on the fact that I have to make this next putt or I'd make a triple-bogey on the hole, which is a worse score. This type of thinking puts even more pressure on you and is not beneficial to the next shot. Compare this approach to one in which you focus all of your effort and energy on the "next shot" or the "next play," while forgetting about anything that happened before, good or bad. This is easier said than done, but with the right guidance and practice, we can help our children to adopt this mentality to stay in the present moment.

To me, the real and perceived adversity our kids will face while playing sports is invaluable experience and may shape how our kids deal with adverse situations in their future. A key part of this is the parental involvement to support and guide every step of the way by pointing out key lessons and create comparisons to future situations they might encounter in their lives.

Humility

No one likes a sore loser and even worse one who is obnoxious when they win. As adults, most of us have encountered people in our lives who have big egos, are self-centered and seem to have the "disease of me." These tend to be people who no one likes and can't stand to be around. Compare this to the people who you've come across who continually deflect praise onto others or show humility, even when they've achieved an accomplishment or level of success. The latter tends to be person held in higher regard and has many friends and advocates. Sportsmanship is a value that can be learned and is often practiced in youth sports. Teaching kids how to be a "good sport" will help them develop humility throughout their lives.

Participation in youth sports will provide our kids exposure to countless scenarios where they will experience both winning and losing. While I was growing up and playing sports, I remember a common practice where both teams always lined up after a game and shook hands. Getting in line, approaching the other team and saying "good game" to every opponent as you shook their hand, regardless of who won or lost, was customary. When I coach I make sure my teams learn to take the opportunity to congratulate their opponent if they won and to say "good game" if they lost. I still see many teams do this at the youth level, but I've also seen plenty of instances where players at higher levels in sports don't always model the best example.

I remember watching a college football game between Penn State and Maryland in 2014 where the captains for both teams met before the game. Typically, the captains from both teams will come together to shake hands before the game as a gesture of sportsmanship. In this case, Maryland's captains refused to shake the hands of the Penn State captains and the announcers pointed it out right away. This sparked a controversy and made the ESPN highlights, leading to widespread discussion of the topic by the public. I think Maryland's coach regretted the incident and the players themselves expressed regret. This situation may have only briefly damaged the reputation of those who were involved, but it was front and center for a national audience to see.

My household watches a lot of collegiate and professional level sports on T.V. and you don't have to look very hard to find athletes who are showboating, dancing, pounding their chest or performing other acts that are self-promoting. Our kids see this, and in many cases, they may look up to some of these athletes as heroes. It's only natural that kids want to emulate or mimic those they admire. With this in mind, we tend to see examples of these behaviors creeping into sports at the youth, middle school and high school levels.

Kids at a young age don't have great impulse control so if something doesn't go their way, they may lash out or have some sort of explosive reaction. I remember a time when my son was 3-years-old and he was playing in his first T-Ball league. When the other team was taking turns batting, the kids out in the field flocked to the ball when it was hit. It became a melee and the kids wrestled one another to be the first to the ball. In one particular instance, my son became so upset that some other kid got the ball. My son slammed his glove on the ground and started crying. During the car ride home, and after the fact ,I had multiple chats with him to explain that he won't always get the ball and that he can't react that way when he doesn't get what he wants.

Having these types of conversations with a three-year-old could be compared to banging your head against a wall, but over time the message started to sink in. The point is that as our kids get older we can always look for those "teachable moments." If we see our kids pointing their hand up to the sky after hitting a homerun, pounding their chest or dancing after they catch a touchdown pass, this is the perfect time to teach them what it means to be humble in victory. Teaching our kids to always shake hands with other teams, respect authority figures, lend support to a teammate who is struggling or even something as simple as handing the referee the ball after a good play, are all ways we can teach our kids humility.

Character

When we encounter well-mannered and respectful children in everyday life we know it was not an accident that they act in this manner. These kids are almost certainly being raised by parents who create a culture where manners and good behavior is the norm. In order to help our kids develop strong character, we need to provide constant reinforcement and demonstrate a lot of patience along the way because there will certainly be bumps in the road. Ideally, we're striving to create a culture in the household so kids grow up understanding right from wrong and we're there every step of the way to guide , correct and praise them. To get to this point, takes a lot of time and effort but participation in youth sports can definitely aid parents in this process.

Through sports, kids are exposed to a lot of different scenarios that teach them to follow rules, respect authority, make the right decisions, even when no one is looking, and give them opportunities to stand out by treating people well. There are countless stories of people demonstrating strong character in sports, but there is one in particular that is in the forefront of my mind.

The story is from 2008 and the setting was a college softball game between Western Oregon vs. Central Washington. During the game, a player from one of the teams hit her first career home run over the fence. As she was rounding first base, she tore her anterior cruciate ligament and collapsed. A girl from the opposing team, who happened to be that school's all-time leader in home runs, asked the umpire if it would be okay if she carried her competitor around the bases so the home run would be official. She was allowed to do it and she and another teammate carried their opponent around the bases so the injured player could touch home plate.

Stories like these highlight great examples of people exhibiting great character through sports. This story was aired on ESPN and gained national exposure. These are the types of stories that we want our kids to see, so we can reinforce the value of doing the right thing at all times.

Sometimes individual sports can provide even more of an opportunity to teach integrity to kids than team sports, because individual sports often require a person to regulate his or her own match without having the luxury of a referee. I look at tennis through the lens of attending my college roommate's collegiate tennis matches. I never had any experience playing tennis myself, but as I'd go to watch some of his matches, I was struck by the fact that the players had to officiate themselves. When we see professional tennis on T.V., there is always a line judge that objectively makes the call to confirm if the ball is in or out of bounds. At every other level of tennis, the competitors make the call themselves.

Golf is another sport where there is no scoreboard that's posted. Instead, the players keep their own scores and they're responsible for administering their own penalty strokes based off the "honor system," if they hit a ball out of bounds or into a water hazard. In individual sports, such as golf and tennis, there is a strong understanding of just how important integrity is to those sports so there is an element of trust. A violation of the rules is certainly frowned upon and there is no place in these sports for any type of dishonesty or cheating.

Both team sports and individual sports provide countless situations that can aid parents in helping to build strong character in their children. These lessons can be introduced through the rules of the sport and through the role of the coach. Lessons can also be driven home by the parents seeking out "teachable moments" and helping to tie everything together and reinforce these lessons for their children.

Learning to take coaching

My experience working at different companies, within the corporate sector, leads me to the conclusion those who elevate through the ranks usually have a good coach or mentor and are open to feedback and constructive criticism. This seems obvious, so it's surprising to me to encounter a good number of people who get defensive or uncomfortable when receiving feedback in a business setting. I've found a large majority of people I work with, that have a background in playing organized team sports, tend to embrace or crave feedback and know it's necessary to maximize their potential.

A majority of the best performers in the world rely on some form of coaching or feedback in their quest to maintain or improve their high level of performance. Someone like a Tom Brady or Drew Brees still works regularly with a coach to analyze or adjust their mechanics. These guys are both all-pros and the best in the world at what they do and yet still seek out coaching on a regular basis. Tiger Woods was always working with a swing coach who helped him to refine his mechanics and reach the highest levels during his extended reign of dominance in the sport of golf. Many top performers, regardless of industry, work with someone to either coach or mentor them and know they could not optimize their performance without this frequent feedback.

Regular coaching is the one thing inherent in youth sports. Not only is coaching frequent and common, I can't think of too many other forums where the coaching can be as specific as it is in sports. My experience in playing youth sports and coaching illustrates how all good coaches give very specific, real-time feedback to help their athletes make adjustments so they improve. Participation in youth sports, over the course of many years, helps to condition our kids to expect and want to be coached and can become ingrained in who they are.

I referenced a "growth mindset" previously in this book and to me embracing coaching and feedback is an example of displaying this type of mindset. Seeking out feedback, in the spirit of continuous improvement, is a key factor that is necessary in the pursuit of excellence. I think that the frequency in which our kids are exposed to feedback and coaching while they are growing up playing sports helps them to establish a lifelong reputation of being coachable.

In business, and in everyday life, I have encountered my fair share of people who have more of a "fixed mindset." These individuals tend to be more accepting of the notion that "they are the way they are" or their current conditions can't be changed. In addition, I come across people who like to tout themselves as being in business or in their current career for 20 or more years and because of this experience, people should just accept them as experts. In reality, things are changing around us all the time and those who fall back on what they've always known, or are not open to new ideas , tend to get passed by and are considered less relevant in the workplace.

Therefore, if youth sports expose kids to regular coaching and feedback and if it conditions these kids to accept coaching and constructive feedback, we can expect they will have an advantage in their professional endeavors. A major role parents can play is to intentionally seek out scenarios that reinforce some of these key lessons to help their kid's development through participating in youth sports. This concept is a recurring theme throughout the book.

Life can be full of ups and downs, but the ability to draw upon scenarios we encountered in our youth, can certainly help us to better handle adversity and also to experience future success with grace and humility. I am passionate about all of the content in this book, but if I had to prioritize my favorite part of the youth sports experience it would be the valuable lessons learned that ultimately enrich the lives of our children.

5

Teaching Leadership Skills

Earlier, I mentioned the lessons that can be drawn from our kids' experience in youth sports. I decided to devote an entire section on leadership, as it requires many qualities and years of practice to master. I remember taking leadership courses in college as part of the curriculum for my major. Through these classes, I learned about the theory of leadership but some lessons did not resonate with me fully because I didn't have the practical experience to draw from. It wasn't until years later when I combined years of practical experience with additional education on the subject that I got to the point where I started to make progress as a leader. I believe leadership is a state of mind and not necessarily a position or a title. There are things we can do for our kids, while playing sports, which can help to instill a leadership mindset.

Leading by Example

There are five leadership concepts I will review in this chapter. These concepts include leading by example, sharing the dream with the team, adopting a growth mindset, empowering others and the power of praise.

Of the five concepts I've mentioned, leading by example and the power of praise are the two we can practice with our kids regardless of their age. Some of the other concepts can become more relevant as our kids get older and continue to progress in sports. Leading by example can take many forms, but we'll look at some of the ways our kids can work on this skill throughout their development.

Teaching kids to "hustle" on the field is something that can help differentiate themselves from other kids at a very young age. In my experience of coaching and umpiring, I have seen plenty of examples where kids might hit a ground ball and just assume they'll be thrown out so they half-heartedly run down the first baseline. In most cases the routine play is made by the opposition and they'll probably be thrown out at first base, regardless of how fast they run. The few instances where the other team bobbles the ball, or makes an error and allows the runner to reach the base safely, are reasons why it's important to hustle at all times during the game.

Recently, Bryce Harper, one of the brightest stars in Major League baseball, was confronted by his teammate Jonathan Papelbon for "loafing" or not hustling on the field. In the age of social media, such scenarios can go viral very quickly. The cameras captured Papelbon confronting Harper in the dugout because Papelbon took offense to his teammate's lack of effort. This is just one of many examples kids might see when watching sports on T.V. This is why it's so important for parents to support the coaches in reinforcing the mindset of moving on the field, so they become second nature. Once a child becomes a known "hustler" or has a reputation of going "all-out," it can rub off on teammates and is a way to lead by example.

"Hustle" can be another term for giving maximum effort. Our kids and the other kids on their teams will all vary in ability, but we can teach our kids to compete with themselves by constantly giving their best effort regardless of what others are doing. Those who are dialed in and aware of the level of effort they are giving, will get noticed by others and stand out as giving their all.

It's important to lead by example with our kids and we can do this in simple ways kids will understand. One example is making it a priority to be punctual and possibly arrive early for their practices and games and explain to our kids the importance of being prompt.

Parents need to lead the way and effectively model the behaviors we expect of our kids so they learn to treat everyone with respect regardless of the setting. If your kids play sports long enough, they'll encounter rude parents, teammates, opponents and opposing coaches on a fairly regular basis. Parents who scream at their kids or at officials can become "white noise" to me because this behavior tends to be so common during games. When kids see their parents behaving this way, they may think it's acceptable and may adopt the same behaviors. Teaching kids to be respectful of coaches, teammates, referees and opponents goes a long way.

If our kids are still playing sports in high school, the demonstration of leading by example might take on other forms such as not drinking or smoking because they don't want to cheat the team. Maybe it looks like working hard on their studies and their grades because they want to be eligible to play, not only their own sake, but for the sake of the team. Avoiding temptation and putting the team first, is a selfless act and an advanced method of leading that respected members of the team display.

There are countless opportunities we can teach our kids to establish fundamentals for leadership by leading through our words and our actions. In the workplace, it's far too common to see a boss who "barks" orders or tells employees what needs to be done. Conversely, the experience feels a lot different if you've worked for a boss who is a great leader and regularly "rolls up his or her sleeves" and works side-by-side with you to accomplish difficult goals. We can help to instill this trait in our kids from a young age and youth sports are a great way to gain practical experience in this important area.

Share your dream with the team

The visionary of the team is usually the role of the coach or a designated leader, but there are various ways that team members can help to share and support a compelling vision. Maybe your child isn't the most talented player on the team, but that doesn't mean he or she isn't capable of emerging as a leader. If your child shows they're one of the hardest workers and shares the vision, they may become a respected member in the group.

Your child might be able to seek out a few other like-minded teammates and create a de facto committee that meets outside of organized practice or games to come up with goals for what the team would like to accomplish during the season. The committee's goal might not be to have the best record in the league or win the championship, but instead be striving to become close to one another as teammates, maximize the team's potential and to have fun while playing! Due to this level of involvement, this sub group of teammates might have a better chance of enlisting support from their teammates beyond what even the coaches can do.

Inspiring a vision within a team might be more realistic for kids as they get older and become more confident in speaking in front of their teammates. Or maybe they get selected as a team captain, which would provide them a more appropriate platform to be vocal about what they'd like to see for their team. Eventually, becoming a team captain could be a realistic goal for our kids to strive for some day. Some kids think only the best players end up being the captain of a team, but in many cases other kids nominate or elect a teammate that is the hardest worker and most supportive member of the team to represent them. If nominated or elected to be a captain on a team, our kids can take advantage of the leadership platform to practice some of these important concepts that can help them to develop into a leader with specific skills they will use in adulthood.

It is much more powerful if individuals from a peer group achieve consensus on the vision or mission for the team. If this occurs, kids tend to police themselves and they'll give much more of themselves to sacrifice for the greater good for the team. Team members tend to hold each other accountable, if they see team members doing something that violates a team rule or policy and is detrimental to the team.

Coaches and parents can play key roles in developing this type of a culture within a team. Some coaches take an "it's my way or the highway" type of approach and expect kids to do everything they're instructed to do without questioning things. Conversely, coaches who select the hardest working and most respected members of a team, to create a compelling vision for their team,

can task this committee to gain buy-in from the rest of their team members.

If the culture of a team is strong enough, parents may find they might not need to worry as much about some of the typical outside influences or temptations many kids struggle with as they reach adolescence. I've personally seen some teams where kids abstained from alcohol, drugs and other potentially common temptations because it would negatively affect their training or preparation. These substances can keep kids from being the best version of themselves and hinder their ability in supporting the team's vision.

Don't get me wrong, the primary responsibility falls upon parents to make sure their kids are growing up to be respectable members of society, but having our kids participate in sports and teams where there's accountability to the group can certainly aid a parent in raising responsible kids. It takes intentional leadership from parents and coaches to help foster an environment where our kids buy into the vision and culture of the team and help them understand how vital their role is on the team. Once this culture has been established, the behaviors tend to naturally fall in line and our kids can learn valuable lessons in leadership along the way.

Adopt a growth mindset

Many have heard the old English proverb, "Necessity is the mother of invention." To me this applies to a team environment when members of a team believe in a team's vision or mission to the point where they will try anything to improve, and get creative, in their pursuit of excellence. It is amazing to see extraordinary things happen when a group of individuals put their heads and hearts together and truly commit to achieving greatness on some level. It's really cool to see some of the innovative ideas that begin to emerge when a team of people are so fully committed in a cause, that they are undeterred.

As our kids grow in their youth sports career, they might assume more of a natural leadership role within the team environment. They may start to challenge processes in the spirit of helping the group to achieve their ultimate mission. At a younger age, we can support the development of a growth mindset in our children by helping them question or be curious. Kids are naturally curious, but somewhere along the way that curiosity tends to be stifled and kids may be conditioned to just accept things as status quo.

We can encourage kids to use their brains and assess what is working and what is not. What are their strengths and weaknesses? How can they strive to get better in areas that are not their strengths? We can also encourage our kids to try something new. Maybe seek out a new drill, that we can turn into a game that also helps to improve a skillset in a certain area. When kids are younger, we can help find fun ways to help them practice and get better so it never feels like a chore.

Teaching kids to challenge processes, whether it's their own processes or those in a group setting, is a valuable skill to acquire and is a trait of strong leaders. This doesn't mean to blatantly challenge authority or purposely not listen to parents and coaches but instead to look at things and ask ourselves if there is a better way to do it. This approach will serve our kids very well as they get older. Adopting this type of mindset gives them an inherent advantage as they get more and more practice in learning to lead others.

As parents, we can aid this process by providing praise and recognition that is more effort or process oriented, rather than outcome oriented. Instead of saying "you're so smart" or "you're such a good athlete," we might say "I like the way you kept practicing and working hard even when you kept missing the ball, or "I know you didn't get that math problem correct but I like how you wouldn't give up and you kept trying." This type of approach can help kids develop grit and embrace struggle or hard work. If they're always put on a pedestal and think of themselves as smart or athletic, they may have a harder time dealing with adversity when they struggle in school or sports for the first time.

Empowering Others

Empowering others can lead to increased engagement or enjoyment in any activity. This is something effective leaders do very well and is a skill that can take a lot of practice. Why not use youth sports as an avenue for our kids to learn this valuable skill that will help them emerge as young leaders as they grow older?

Coaches can create this type of environment by rotating different responsibilities, such as having different kids lead the stretching at the beginning of practice or coordinate the cleanup efforts at the end of practice. Another idea is to have the coach pick a different member of the team to choose an inspirational quote to share before each practice or game. A coach could also assign a rotating team member to lead the team cheer at the end of practice or games. Also, team members who are not currently getting playing time can keep track of the statistics for his or her teammates. There are a lot of creative ways coaches and parents can encourage engagement, which can ultimately lead to a more fulfilling experience.

We can also teach our kids to keep an eye out for teammates who are less confident and encourage our kids to assist their teammates and "take them under their wing." This can be done at a very young age and it's a great way to help teach our kids Emotional Intelligence (EI), which will help increase their awareness of other people's feelings. An example of this would be to encourage our kids to make friends with someone on the team who is shy and quiet or be supportive when a teammate seems down because of an error he or she might have made.

Teaching our kids to connect with disengaged teammates is a valuable skill to learn, that can become second nature for our kids if parents are intentional about it at an early age. As our kids get older, and are playing at more competitive levels, connecting with teammates in a manner that creates greater engagement can only help increase team cohesion, ultimately benefitting the team.

In leadership positions in the business realm, I've discovered empowering others, by enabling them to act, is a powerful way to increase engagement. Increased engagement leads to getting the best version of the individuals who make up the team and helps in reaching the maximum potential of a group. This increased engagement has a compounding effect and teams that reach this level are usually teams that achieve the most and meet their goals.

The Power of Praise

The final leadership-based concept I'll cover is teaching our kids to find opportunities to praise and recognize their teammates. At the beginning of this chapter I mentioned leading by example and the power of praise are two concepts that are the easiest to teach and execute, even at the youngest levels of youth sports.

We can teach our kids to be beacons of positivity by always having a kind or supportive word to say to teammates during practices and games. I've seen coaches establish team building activities designed to create bonds between team members they're coaching. One idea is for the coach to hand out a brief questionnaire for the kids to fill out, with the help of their parents, to list the kids' likes, dislikes and favorites things etc. At the end of the next practice, the kids can all pair up with another teammate to learn about each other and then share with the rest of the group. This can help the kids to connect and bond with one another. It can also be a valuable tool for coaches and teammates to find ways to customize recognition or praise that is meaningful for all team members.

As parents, we can reinforce ideas and run through scenarios with our kids on the way to practice or during the car ride home after games. During this time we can cover situations we observed might be an appropriate time for our child to offer praise or recognition to a teammate. If we are constantly reinforcing how our kids can be a supportive teammate, and find ways to "catch people doing things right," this awareness may become second nature and they will gain invaluable practice to become great leaders.

It can be easy to find ways to recognize or praise teammates, who do great things, but it can take more effort and diligence to find ways to offer support to a teammate who may have let the team down. When growing up playing youth sports, I can remember certain moments when an action or inaction of mine may have hurt the team or contributed to a loss.

Making an error at a crucial moment or striking out with the bases loaded that ends the game, can have a memorable impact on a child. It's amazing how years later, events like this still stick in our memory. When something like this happens a child can feel alone or isolated from the group. The natural way for teammates to cope might be to avoid the situation or say nothing at all to the team member who had the bad experience. Situations like this can be awkward and other kids might not know what to say so they choose to not say anything at all.

Providing support and recognition in these instances can go a long way. We can teach our kids to give praise to teammates who do something very well and also teach them to find meaningful ways to offer condolences to a teammate who might feel bad after making a blunder. If the kids are friends, this might mean calling them after the game or stopping by their house to offer support privately. Teaching kids to be aware of the feelings of others will only help to increase their Emotional Intelligence when they are young, which has been shown in certain studies to be one of the main determinants of success for an adult.

Teaching kids to provide praise and support to teammates and friends can be the easiest and most fun concepts of leadership. This concept still takes practice in order for this skill to become second nature. Our role as parents is to use our experience to help our children seek out situations where it might be appropriate to praise or support others.

There is research that suggests participation in youth sports can enhance children's ability to display leadership skills and possibly hold leadership positions. A 2015 report published in the Journal of Leadership and Organizational Studies, entitled "Sports at Work: Anticipated and Persistent Correlates of Participation in High School Athletics," sheds some light on this notion. The authors of the study completed two complementary studies that attempted to gauge whether or not former student-athletes made better employees. In the first study, a sampling of 66 adults was asked questions to learn how the participants perceived people who participated in extracurricular activities while in high school. The second study used data from 931 World War II veterans to determine how participation in youth sports may have influenced the veteran's career paths, leadership skills and the likelihood they'd donate to charity. Some of the key findings of the study include the following:

- People tend to expect former student-athletes to display higher levels of leadership, self-confidence and self-respect than former students who participated in the school band or school yearbook club during school.
- Of the veterans who were surveyed, those who played at least one varsity sport in high school tended to rate higher scores in categories related to leadership, self-confidence and self-respect than those who did not.

• Former student-athletes were more likely to report they do volunteer work and donate money to various organizations more than 55 years after graduating from high school.

• A larger proportion of former student-athletes reported having had careers in "upper management."

As I reflect back on my on my own life, and especially my professional career, I find it has been the years of hands-on experience and practice that has helped me to make strides in becoming a better leader. I've taken college courses on the subject, read articles and books and yet it's the practical application of the concepts that has helped the most. Why not treat youth sports as a platform to help expose our children to and practice some of these important leadership lessons? The above- mentioned studies indicate leadership tends to come more naturally for those who have grown up playing youth sports. As parents, we can certainly be intentional about how we solidify some of these leadership practices in our children's minds, which may help to expedite the process and help them to become better leaders at an earlier age.

The exposure to these benefits, while participating in youth sports, gives kids a lot of practice and a definite head start in embracing these philosophies so they become natural over time. In almost any occupation or livelihoods, our kids might pursue, these lessons may help them tremendously to become stronger leaders. As parents, we can have fun while we guide our kids along the way and help fuel their development.

6

The Case Against Specialization

In the last couple of decades, there has been a shift of emphasis toward "elite" competition in youth sports. The Washington Post recently reported between 2009-2014, youth sports participation, in general, is down 4% and the total number of sports played is down by about 10%. When kids are specializing in one sport and playing in year-round leagues, there is minimal time left to participate in other sports, which explains the drop-off in the number of total youth sports played.

With youth sports becoming such big business, parents, coaches and league administrators seem to be steering kids to specialize in one sport. The thought behind this is if kids show promise in a particular sport, their talent can be maximized if they devote all of their time and attention to that one sport. You also see people who are making a living as quarterback gurus or instructors; pitching coaches or they might open up a performance enhancement facility. This growing contingency of performance gurus are promoting the specialization direction that youth sports are heading. Training has become more specialized that it can give the false notion to parents who think if their child doesn't play on the travel/elite team, or go to the top instructor in the area, their child might be left behind in their particular sport.

I was playing youth sports in the early 1980s and my parents allowed me to play many different organized sports. This level of exposure helped me to develop a well-rounded enjoyment of most sports, which I still carry with me to this day. I do remember playing on a travel soccer team in Ohio for a few years that was very competitive for my age group. There were intense tryouts for this team and it felt really good to not only make the team, but to be a regular contributor to the success of the team.

I remember taking a trip to Notre Dame for a tournament, which was definitely one of the highlights of my youth sports career. At the time, I didn't realize the expense and additional burden this placed on my family but the trips were prerequisite for being a member of the team. I recently read an article in Forbes magazine by Bud Cook, who stated "an estimated 27% of all family trips are taken solely for an organized sporting event." Parents not only have to spend their hard earned money on this type of travel, they also have to use burn their valuable vacation time for these trips instead of traditional family vacations.

The head coach of my soccer team was a good coach, but he had very little tolerance for his players playing multiple sports at the same time. I remember my baseball season overlapped with my soccer season and some nights I would have to go to more than one practice. I remember asking my coach if it would be okay if I could leave practice a little early so I could make it to my baseball practice. At one point, my coach said I needed to choose one sport and give my full commitment to that sport.

I don't remember my exact age when this conversation took place, but I had to be somewhere in the range of 8 to 10-years-old. Looking back, it seems selfish to me that a coach would encourage a kid this age to choose only one sport and stick to just that. This happened prior to the movement toward specialization, but it wasn't too many years later where travel and elite teams started to become more and more prevalent. With that came the expectation if a child plays on a year-round travel team, he or she should give 100% of their extra time and energy to that sport.

The travel and elite teams one of the main reasons why youth sports have become such big business. The same Forbes article I referenced also went on to cover the realization that spending in youth sports appeared to be recession proof during the economic downturn of 2007-2009. The author of the article went on to say organizations that are in the business of attracting travel teams to towns around the country, report there are roughly 53 million youth sports participants, resulting in $7 billion in annual spending.

Aside from the financial burden some travel teams create for families, steering kids toward one sport specialization, at such an early age, can affect their love of sports. If I had not grown up playing basketball, baseball, football, golf etc., I might not have the overall appreciation for sports that I do today. I remember playing all of these sports, and more, in my driveway and backyard with all of my neighborhood friends. We would play for hours on end and often times had to be summoned by our parents to come in for dinner because it was dark outside. Even though I might not have been the best at any of those sports, exposure to all of them allowed me to become a well-rounded athlete, learn cross-functional movements, develop better hand-eye coordination and learn various sets of rules to different sports.

Keith Van Horn, an All American basketball player at the University of Utah, played in the NBA for 10 years and currently sits on the board of the Positive Coaching Alliance, which is an organization that prides itself on highlighting some of the positive virtues and principles of sports. In his blog, "Layups and Rebounds," he recalled an experience when his daughter tried out and made one of the top 5th grade teams in their state and the coach of that team demanded his daughter specialize in basketball. If she were to decide to play for the team, she would have to make a one year commitment to play only that sport on that team. The coach went on to tell him that all of the best players were specializing in basketball in 5th or 6th grade and if his daughter did not focus on this sport, she would fall behind and it might jeopardize her ability to earn a college scholarship.

Can you imagine a coach having the audacity to tell a father who played at the highest collegiate and professional levels of the same sport what he needs to do to enhance his daughter's chances for success in that sport? If a coach is willing to speak with that type of conviction to someone who played that sport at the highest levels, imagine how much influence a coach like that might have on your typical parent. It's no wonder we've seen such a migration to one sport specialization at earlier and earlier ages.

There is evidence that suggests year-round exposure to playing the same sport, with the same movements over and over, can lead to repetitive use injuries in kids. The beauty of learning and playing different sports is kids are forced into different movement patterns, which helps to develop a wide array of different muscle groups and skill sets. Travel baseball teams come to mind when I think of young kids with injuries, specifically arm injuries. Some teams are so competitive, and have such a "win at all cost mentality," that if one kid is the team's star pitcher, there is a good chance an overzealous coach will pitch this player more frequently than is safe for the player. Even in the Major Leagues, starting pitchers typically need at least 4 or 5 days of rest to prevent injury and promote maximum recovery.

John Smoltz, who was a very successful pitcher for the Atlanta Braves, had some strong comments about avoiding one sport specialization during his induction speech when he entered the Major League Baseball Hall of Fame. Smoltz had to undergo Tommy John surgery, or ulnar collateral ligament (UCL) reconstruction surgery, to repair an injury to his pitching arm. Today, this surgery is more prevalent for Major League pitchers. It's gotten to the point where Tommy John surgery is becoming so common it's almost thought of as a band aid for one's arm. At this point, John Smoltz is the only pitcher who has made it to the Hall of Fame after having this surgery.

Smoltz went on to talk about how it is not normal for anyone's child to need Tommy John surgery at age 14 or 15. He also said "baseball is not a year-round sport and our children should play other sports, which can prevent overuse. Every pitch our kids throw should not be a competitive pitch to where they are 'maxing out.'" Kids should be able to play recreationally and with friends in an environment that is not always structured. Smoltz also stated, "Don't let the institutions that are out there running before you guaranteeing scholarship dollars and signing bonuses tell you that this is the way..." Smoltz seems to be passionate about how encouraging kids to specialize in one sport is absolutely leading to a rise in injuries, especially in a sport like baseball.

Overall, the shift to specialization in sports through so called "elite" teams has taken a toll on those who have embraced this approach. Specializing athletes, at too young an age, is not only affecting their love of sports, but it's not even a proven method of improving one's skill in a particular sport. Many parents who urge their son or daughter to excel in one sport, have found this strategy may actually backfire because of injury, strained mental stamina, underdevelopment of other muscles and lack of enjoyment. There is more and more evidence that children who end up playing multiple sports tend to reach higher levels of achievement and success in sports on a more consistent basis.

The National Football League happens to be the undisputed most popular sport in America when measured by T.V. ratings, fan bases, merchandising etc. This popularity has more and more children growing up as fans of the NFL and wanting to play football at an early age. NFL branded flag football leagues are popping up all over the country and allowing participation as early as five years old. These leagues give kids access to wear uniforms that are branded in their favorite NFL team names and colors. To go along with this popularity, you see more and more specialized training for kids to learn to be quarterbacks or other position-specific types of training.

What's interesting is NFL.com reported that out of the 2015 class of players that were drafted into the NFL, 224 of the 256 players grew up playing multiple sports. That means that nearly

88% of the players drafted, to play the most popular sport in our country, grew up playing more than just football.

Now, let's take a look at last year's college football National Champions. Urban Meyer is the highly successful head coach of the 2015 National Champion Ohio State Buckeyes team and it seems he has a preference to recruit kids who grew up playing multiple sports. According to OK Preps, a chart that went viral on the Internet conveyed that of the 47 athletes Urban Meyer had recruited to play at Ohio State, 42 of them played multiple sports in high school. That's roughly 89% of his players who had a background playing other sports beyond football.

We can also look at other areas outside of football. The Olympics are representative of many different athletes who compete at the highest levels, across many different sports. In 2014, the United States Olympic Committee completed a comprehensive survey of all recent Olympians and found the Olympic competitors played an average of three sports per year, between the ages of 10 to 14 and they averaged just over two sports per year between the ages of 15 to18. I know my own perception was that most Olympic athletes grew up specializing in their sport from the time they were very young. These findings prove my perception, and that of others, as outdated or just plain inaccurate.

There are clear exceptions to this rule, when we think of people like Andre Agassi, Venus and Serena Williams, Tiger Woods and

Todd Marinovich, just to name a few. These are examples of people who were groomed for their respective sport at a very young age and ended up reaching the highest levels of that sport, which ended up becoming their profession. For every story where kids reached the pinnacle of their sport through specialization, there are countless other stories of kids who may have quit their sport because they were burned out or injured. As a matter of fact, Andre Agassi and Todd Marinovich have shared, after their playing careers were over, about the pressures they felt to be successful and how it affected their ability to have a normal childhood.

College coaches may have various reasons for wanting to recruit kids who have grown up playing multiple sports. For many coaches, recruiting athletes who grew up playing more than one sport ensures they are bringing well-rounded players onto their teams, who have had the opportunity to develop different skill sets. This approach may also indicate there is a greater likelihood the kids are coachable.

Bobby Knight, who was one of the most successful college basketball coaches of all-time, has gone on record to say it was part of his recruiting process to watch kids play their secondary sports because it would tell him a lot about the player's overall ability. If he was recruiting a star basketball player, he might attend one of the athlete's football or baseball games. He would watch body language or try to get a gauge on the athlete's attitude. Being in a position where the player will not be the star player on a team is a different dynamic that could provide insight to determine if that athlete possesses humility.

It might also give him an idea of how hard that athlete is willing to work when he is playing a sport that might not come as natural. Watching an athlete play another sport can create a scenario where the athlete is not put on a pedestal or constantly praised and this might also reveal what type of team player they are or how they handle adversity. This seems like a smart approach and clearly served Knight well on his way to achieving over 900 wins during his career as a head basketball coach.

Jordan Spieth is an athlete who spent most of the 2015 PGA golf season in the spotlight with strong play that led him to win the 2015 player of the year award. According to an article title "Athlete first," published by the Titleist Performance Institute, Spieth grew up playing football, basketball and baseball, in addition to playing golf. The article went on to say Spieth excelled in golf at a very young age and by the time he was twelve-years-old, he asked his parents if he could stop playing other sports so he could concentrate only on golf. His parents knew he loved golf and was really good at it, but they had the foresight to encourage him to continue to play some of the other team sports where he excelled.

Spieth's mom, Chris, shared her thoughts in an interview with purpose2play.com, where she shared, "There's a lot that can be learned from competing as a team. I think having that experience really grounds you and prepares you for other things in life beyond sports. I think, sometimes, when kids show an aptitude for golf at a young age, their parents push them into spending all of their time on that one sport. They get burnt out and they don't have the opportunity to explore all of the other things out there." Chris had strong feelings there was a lot for her son to learn and experience by playing team sports and carry on those lessons throughout his life. Spieth's younger brother, Steven, went on to play Division I college basketball at Brown University, which is further evidence to me that Spieth's parents really tried to expose their kids to all sports and learn what their kids might be passionate about, before specializing in one sport.

A final example is Ryan McDonagh, who is an athlete at the top of his sport and attributes a lot of his success to playing multiple sports. Ryan is the captain of the New York Ranger hockey team and he not only tried other sports while he was growing up, but he played them at a very high level. The high school baseball team that Ryan played on won a state championship and Ryan was also an all-state level player on his high school football team. In an article in Parents Magazine, author David Sparrow Ryan was quoted as saying, "Playing other sports was good for my hand-eye coordination and strength. And it was positive socially, too: I hung out with a bunch of friends who played each sport. There is so much out there for your kids to explore, and you should let them."

Hopefully, we have covered enough testimonials to at least plant the seed of doubt next time a coach or league administrator tries to "sell" you on why it's important for your kids to specialize in one sport. It's important to be aware of what college coaches look for when recruiting athletes for their teams. It's also good to know the make-up of professional sports rosters with a vast majority of players who reached the professional level by playing multiple sports while growing up. These facts directly counter the messages our children are hearing, which are leading to more one sport specialization. We can also tie it back to the earlier chapter on participation. It is not possible for our kids to experience all of the great benefits of youth sports if they end up quitting because they've become burned out from playing one sport all year round.

7

The Unifying Power of Sports

I f your children happen to participate in youth sports without quitting at an early age, they will more than likely have been exposed to the myriad of benefits I've discussed up to this point. It is also probable they'll have developed a love for sports that will last throughout their lifetime, whether they go on to compete beyond high school or beyond.

I've also heard of many scenarios where parents enrolled their kids into sports initially, at a young age, even though their parents may not have had an interest or passion for sports. More often than not, parents get so caught up in their child's passions that they begin to enjoy the very same sports they've watched their kids grow up playing. Usually this means a foundation, from a lifetime of shared experiences, has often times been laid. This foundation is evidence of the power that sports can have in unifying different groups of people. The power to bring people together is one of the greatest benefits that come from a love of sports and it can last a lifetime.

Shared Family Sports Experiences

Both of my parents enjoyed sports but I was not brought up in an environment that forced me to play or like sports. My parents gave me the opportunity to experience many different sports and I grew up being aware of the teams, coaches and players that were influential in the lives of my family members. I appreciate my mom's level of sacrifice she made by constantly "carting" me around town, in our Toyota Tercel, to get to various games and practices while, balancing my activities with those of my two other siblings. While growing up, it was pretty normal for my brother and I to play, practice and hone our skills at the different sports we liked. We did this because we loved to and not because somebody was forcing us to.

I can remember my brother and me dragging our poor sister outside to practice in our attempt to "prepare" her for softball practices and games. I remember many of the names of the coaches of both my teams and my brother and sister's teams during our childhood. Many of these experiences, in general, helped shape me into the person I've become and fueled my continued passion for sports today. When family members have similar interests in sports or teams it can be a great way to share experiences that will be enjoyed over the course of a lifetime.

I can remember as young boys, my dad had my brother and I trained to give the right answer when he would chant the phrase "We Are!" and we would respond with "Penn State!" at the top of our lungs. That was just one of the many mantras, cheers or phrases I grew up with and still remember and practice today. I also remember when my dad started taking my brother and me to our beloved Pittsburgh Steelers games, when we were around eight or nine years old. My brother and I would get so excited to attend games at old Three Rivers Stadium and root for our favorite players through all kinds of weather, and Steeler wins and losses. I remember our family hopelessly staying to the end of a 51-0 blowout when the Steelers got dominated by the Cleveland Browns, in the much-anticipated season opener of the 1989 season. I can still feel the bone chilling cold we felt when we were at the 2001 AFC Championship between the Steelers and Patriots in sub-zero temperatures.

My point in bringing up these memories is to further illustrate how shared experiences through sports can stay with us for years. I think I have an average memory, but it's amazing how my ability to recall the vivid details of some of these events is so much greater than other experiences that fade into the depths of my mind. I hope to create these same types of memories with both of my children so they have positive associations of family and sports intertwined and can draw upon those memories years later.

As an adult I now live in Phoenix, Arizona, which is far away from most of my family who still reside back in the Midwest. I think I do a decent job of keeping in touch with my family and friends, both by phone and email, on a regular basis. It's amazing to see how the frequency of contact increases quite a bit during certain times of the year that coincide with sports seasons. I tend to talk to both my dad and brother a lot more when football season starts and we find ourselves either recapping a Steelers or Penn State game. Other times we call each other to share our thoughts and opinions of what we think our teams' chances are heading into a big game. It's not uncommon to spend a good portion of my conversations, with both my mom and my grandma, about the sporting teams we share a common interest and support of a team.

As my wife and I raise our young son and daughter, we find ourselves teaching them some of the same phrases, mantras and fight songs we grew up learning and it has become a bridge between generations in my family. I do not believe in forcing any of my interests on my kids but I also believe in cultural assimilation. Kids really enjoy spending good quality time with their parents and in doing so, they can pick up similar interests and passions that can lay the foundation for a lifetime of positive associations and shared experiences.

Forging Unbreakable Bonds with Teammates

I can think of countless examples of teammates who were part of successful teams that have created very strong bonds with those whom they shared blood, sweat and tears with during their time playing together. One of the best things about organized sports is the camaraderie, team spirit and trust that are developed for team members who share successes and adversity while accomplishing things that are bigger than any one individual could accomplish.

I recently read a book I would recommend to anyone called, "Boys in the Boat." This book is a true story of a crew team at the University of Washington that overcame many odds to win the Gold Medal in the 1936 Berlin Olympics. I did not know much about the sport of crew prior to reading this book, but the author was so descriptive in telling the story I not only feel like I have a better understanding of the sport, but I shared in some of the highs and lows the main characters felt in their quest to make it to the Olympic games.

In this book, the head coach of the University of Washington's rowing team tinkered with different lineups and combinations over the course of a couple years before he finally settled on a team of eight student athletes who really enjoyed each other's company and trusted one another. The interesting thing was each of the boys, individually, may not have been the fastest or the strongest but collectively, they all had strengths and skillsets that complemented one another very well and led to a cohesive team. Once the team really started to bond, they started to make their historic run, which culminated in the gold medal at the 1936 Olympic Games in Berlin, Germany.

One of the things that stood out to me, other than the buildup and suspense that led to the Olympics, was the author's account of how the team members stayed in touch over the years. The team members would organize reunions they continued until most of them grew old and passed away. For milestone reunions, they even went as far as to coordinate team rows where they would all get in the boat in similar positions when they rowed on the Olympic team. When the living members of the team were interviewed, it was amazing to hear how they, spoke with such reverence for their teammates. The shared experiences and accomplishments they created as teammates unified them forever.

Another story comes to mind from my own circle of influence that illustrates how shared memories and accomplishments can really bond teammates together even years after the event took place. The setting was around 1995 when the Boardman Spartans upset the St. Ignatius Wildcats in a high school football matchup. My brother played for Boardman, a team prepared to take on St Ignatius that was a perennial powerhouse in Division I Ohio high school football. Ignatius had won many state championships and was riding a historic 38-game winning streak when my brother's team prepared to play against them.

Ignatius had a lot more talent and size than Boardman's team and on paper this was quite a lopsided matchup. My brother was a perfect example of an overachiever, who had finally earned his way into a starting position during his senior year. My brother and

I both were naturally small kids, but he had lifted weights and worked very hard at conditioning so he made himself into a decent player by the time he was a senior. His hard work paid off when he was designated as one of the starting linebacker positions on a pretty good defense. I was away at college at the time, but I took a trip home just so I could support him for the biggest game of the season.

As the game unfolded, Ignatius had a big lead and it looked as though they would exert their dominance and run away with the game before the game slowly started to turn. There was a big play early in the second half that shifted the momentum and Boardman came roaring back and ended up barely winning the game, which was played on Boardman's home turf. I can remember all of Boardman's fans rushing the field and joining in on the celebration of a monumental upset. This game ended up being the best game of my brother's playing career, as he had 13 tackles and several other key stops that impacted the game.

Twenty years later, when he happens to run into members of that team, many of them remember it like it was yesterday. They all shared in an experience that was a great accomplishment for them all and one they'll remember with great detail for the rest of their lives. A guy by the name of D.J. Durkin, was a member of that team who has gone on to a highly successful college football coaching career. Durkin made mention of this game to me years later. Durkin was featured in a segment on the popular show

College Gameday, in which he was wearing a microphone on the field during a piece that recognized him as one of the brightest young assistant coaches in college football. I didn't keep in touch with Durkin over the years, but I sent him an email congratulating him on the recognition he got and for the success he had gained as a coach. He very politely e-mailed me back but before his closing, he told me to tell my brother a key hit that he had in the Boardman/Ignatius game, was still one of the best hits he had seen in all of his years in the game of football.

The point of this story is, a guy who has gone on to have a lot of success and is at the pinnacle of his profession, remembers the small details of a shared experience he had with a high school teammate. Many others, who have played organized sports, have similar memories and are memories that continue to unify teammates long after their playing days are over.

The Fan Experience

We see examples of sports teams unifying fans, of all sorts, all over the world through the formation of mini communities that support a favorite sport or team. Soccer is the most popular sport in the world and we see fans and entire countries alike, passionately support their teams. This is very evident every four years during the World Cup where sometimes businesses will be shut down when local or home teams are playing. Some countries are so passionate about their soccer team; it causes behavior that seems absurd to rational people.

There is a bestselling book called "Flow," written by famous psychologist Mihaly Csikszentmihalyi. This book goes into great depth to describe the various ways people attain happiness or optimal experiences. The author states, "The audiences at today's live performances, such as rock concerts, continue to partake in some degree in these ritual elements; there are few other occasions at which large numbers of people witness the same information. Such joint participation produces in an audience the condition Emile Durkheim called collective effervescence, or the sense that one belongs to a group with a concrete, real existence. This feeling, Durkheim believed, was at the roots of religious experience."

This makes perfect sense to me, as I personally have felt this level of enjoyment through attending games to support my favorite teams or through gatherings or "watch parties." A large number of fans who get together to support a team, might be candidates to create this type of effect. The author mentioned rock concerts specifically, but attending a live sporting event has many of the same elements he described. There are definitely ritualistic elements at live sporting events. In many cases there are customs or traditions such as tailgating where people enjoy preparing food and drinks to enhance the overall experience. Fight songs, mantras and team merchandise are just some of what is seen and heard while attending a live sporting event. The notion that collective effervescence can be compared to a sort of religious experience, is something t I have witnessed firsthand throughout the games I have attended in my lifetime.

When I lived in the Midwest, my brother and I had season tickets for Pittsburgh Steelers home games and we went to just about every game we could. I attended the games for years and thoroughly enjoyed those experiences. When I moved across the country to Phoenix, Arizona I was not able to attend those games nearly as often. Missing the games was one of the few drawbacks I felt when moving away. While in Phoenix, I found an establishment called Harold's that just so happens to be one of the largest Steelers "backer" restaurant/bars in the country. Harold's boast the largest number of fan club members of any Steelers backer establishments, outside of Pittsburgh.

This place combines many of the same ritualistic elements fans experience by attending the live games. They have a D.J. who plays Steelers songs including selections they play in the stadium during games. The menu includes items that are known to be served in Pittsburgh. On a weekly basis, Harold's will have over 1,000 Steelers fans visit to watch the Steelers games. In years when the team has made it to the playoffs and the Super Bowl, Harold's had upwards of 5,000 people in attendance.

When I first moved to Phoenix, I paid to reserve the same table every week and I've renewed that membership every year. I have sat with or near the same group of people for the last eight years and this dynamic has helped to transform Harold's to feel like a second family. I look forward to seeing the same people every year when football season rolls around. Harold's incorporates many of the elements that leads to a "flow-like" experience and it does a great job acting as a unifier for large groups of people who have a place where they can gather and feel like they're back home rooting on their team.

Being a fan of sports or similar teams can be a great way for friends and family to stay connected as they grow older. Connecting through sports can help to combat the tendency to lose touch with important people in our lives. Most of us become so busy with our own professional and family lives, we may lose touch. A friend of mine stays in touch with a group of his college buddies, primarily by planning a road trip every year where they choose one Cleveland Browns away game in a city most of them have never visited before. Every year he comes back with great stories, pictures and shared experiences all while keeping in contact with people he has been friends with for years.

I have established my own tradition that allows me to better connect with a group of friends and family members who live in different places across the country. I got married in 2011 and at my wedding, a core group of about eight of my friends and family decided we ought to plan a "Pennsylvania sports weekend" every year. The basis for this trip is to find a weekend when both Penn State and the Pittsburgh Steelers each have a home game on a back-to-back Saturday and Sunday. We planned the first trip and we've now established this tradition that has been going on for four years straight, with plans to continue in the years to come. A shared interest in the sports teams we all root for, has been the impetus for us to create an excuse to travel together and enjoy one another's company. I feel this annual trip has enriched my life and I look forward to seeing these people that I care about on a yearly basis. The sports fan experience is a very natural way to connect various groups of people, friends and strangers alike, and help to establish new and solidify existing relationships.

Communities Unite

Sports can often be a great unifier for entire communities. I attended two different high schools and I follow both schools on various social media platforms. Recently, one of those school's boys' golf team qualified for the Ohio State Golf tournament. I was able to watch some videos of a send-off parade for the team before they left to travel to Columbus. By watching the video, I could see the amount of pride the families, friends, classmates and community members felt for the team and the support they showed was such a nice gesture.

Seeing this video triggered my memories of past experiences in my youth. For example, I can remember entire communities coming together to support the local sports team. I can also remember travelling with my family around to different venues to watch the local high school football team's games as they advanced deep into the state playoffs. The timing of the football playoffs in Ohio tends to coincide with very cold weather, and many times we froze our butts off while watching the games.

Some of these experiences were fun because a large contingency of people travelled to support their hometown team by showing up wearing the colors and gear of the team. Laughs, hugs, handshakes, smiles and at times let-down because of a loss, were all shared by both friends and complete strangers alike. Travelling to support a team everyone cared about seemed to promote a great human connection, as people enjoyed one another while supporting something the same team.

Soon after I moved to Phoenix, towards the end of 2007, the Arizona Cardinals happened to make a deep run into the playoffs and ultimately made it to the Super Bowl. It just so happened they were matched up against the Steelers. A lot of the local hoopla I saw was wasted on me, but I did notice it nonetheless. At this point in time, the Cardinals fan base had been accustomed to years of futility. In fact, the team was one of the worst teams in the league on a pretty consistent basis.

Although it may have been annoying to me, since many of the local fans opposed my team, it was amazing to see a transformation occur across the city of Phoenix. Fans, young and old wore Cardinals gear for the two weeks leading up to the Super Bowl. There were rallies, parties and gatherings that took place all across the Valley of the Sun. I found myself asking fans how long they had been supporters of the Cardinals, in my smug attempt to prove to myself how many people associate with their fan base were fair-weather fans. Many people admitted to me they didn't really like football but they knew this was good for the city so they were spending money on team merchandise and supporting the team for the good of the local economy.

Whether you root for a certain team or not, it's fun to watch a community or a city transform before your eyes, in support of a local team who is doing well. The last example I will share is the effect that one player had on the entire state of Ohio. Lebron James grew up in Northeast Ohio and was arguably the most talked about and publicized young basketball players of all time. Myself and others anxiously watched the NBA lottery the year that Lebron declared for the draft and were thrilled when the ping pong ball fell the Cavs way and, it was evident Lebron was going to be drafted by the hometown team.

The Cavs went from not being a very good team to being a fixture in the playoffs for many years after Lebron joined the team. They made deep playoff runs and even made it to the NBA Finals one year before losing. Cleveland's team became one of the most popular teams in the league, was nationally televised, enjoyed increased merchandising and sold out every game on a consistent basis.

Local businesses, specifically bars and restaurants in downtown Cleveland, thrived because of all of the money injected into their businesses. People near and far came downtown to watch Lebron and the Cavs play because they had become such an attraction.

This stretch was a great time in the Cleveland sports scene and it seemed like the majority of the city really came together in support of the Cavs.

Then it seemed to come all crashing down when Lebron James became a free agent and announced in a T.V. program, called "The Decision," he was leaving Cleveland to take his talents to the Miami Heat. The fallout from this decision was unbelievable. So many of the local fans in the community had hurt feeling over this. The news showed people burning Lebron's jerseys and calling him all kinds of names. I definitely saw the worst side of many people during this time. His departure led to an immediate drop off in performance for the team to the extent the Cavs instantly became one of the worst teams in the league for the next four years. Bars and restaurants in downtown Cleveland suffered, and in some cases, went out of business as they saw their revenues plummet because the Cavs were no longer attracting droves of fans to come downtown to support the team.

Lebron became a free agent again in 2014 and rumors started to surface he might come back to Cleveland. Fans quickly came to terms with forgiving Lebron who had been vilified ever since he left the Cavs four years earlier. When it became official that Lebron came back to Cleveland, fans everywhere rejoiced. For weeks, his was the lead story in national sporting news outlets all over the country. The ticket office phones rang off the hook and all of the home games for the rest of the basketball season were sold out. The T.V. networks decided to air more Cavalier games than any other team during the course of Lebron's return season to his hometown team.

The whole thing became quite a story that culminated with Lebron carrying the Cavs to the NBA finals, where they lost a heartbreaking series to the Golden State Warriors. Despite the loss, the whole season was quite a ride and I've never seen one player have the power to unite a whole city and conversely, polarize a whole city, all within the span of his career. There have been countless articles written that attempt to quantify the economic impact this one player has had on the Cleveland community. In this case, a transcendent superstar player had the ability to bring such a sense of pride and entertainment to an area that is often associated with the hardships of their other local sports teams.

Up to this point in the book, I've covered a lot of the benefits participation in sports can give to our children. I've talked about health benefits, life lessons, leadership and others, and also highlighted how exposure to years of sports can create lifelong sports fans. The stories I've shared in this chapter do not begin to do justice for all the ways sports can create deeper connections and maintain important relationships in our lives. These connections are something I've definitely taken advantage of in my life and I foresee it doing the same for my children for years to come.

8

Intentional Role Models

If all goes according to plan, our kids will enjoy participating in sports and, along the way; they will take advantage of the many benefits that comes along with the experience. In many cases, they'll want to attend games, watch games on T.V. and may gravitate toward certain teams or players. College and professional sports have become so popular athletes and coaches can have an influence on society, especially on young kids who are impressionable.

Many athletes, who make it to the professional ranks, end up overcoming hardship to get there. They might go from having nothing to becoming very wealthy in their early twenties, before they've fully matured as people. This is not always a good formula. Instant fame and wealth, without the maturity to handle it, can lead to poor decisions. Combine this with our abundance of media outlets and being thrust into the limelight, it's hard for these athletes to keep their personal lives private.

In recent years, the media has brought stories to light about athletes associated with drug use, domestic violence, infidelity and irresponsible parenting, just to name a few. Aside from these more serious matters, it does not take much channel surfing to see examples of athletes taunting, berating referees, showboating and acting in ways that are contradictory to some of the life lessons we discussed in Chapter 4. If left to chance, our kids might develop favorite players who don't necessarily showcase the types of actions and behaviors we want our kids imitating.

In this chapter, I will discuss how some athletes and coaches can serve as positive role models for our kids. Our role as parents is to intentionally guide our kids to this type of role model instead of negative role models, who our kids might naturally gravitate towards. This is not to suggest we put anyone on a pedestal or have our kids think these people are perfect, but at the very least we can admire the way that they carry themselves personally and professionally.

The Book of Manning

As a casual fan, I have long admired the way that Peyton and Eli Manning have carried themselves professionally, while in the public eye. Recently, I watched a documentary titled "The Book of Manning," that really gave good insight into the family as a whole and the way that Archie and Olivia Manning raised their three boys. The film depicted the Manning parents as very intentional parents who raised their kids to have strong character and values.

Archie Manning was raised in Mississippi and developed a love for sports at an early age. He grew up in an era where fathers may not have been as outward in expressing their love and affection for their children. Archie seemed to be drawn to sports as a way to bond with his father. Archie was a tremendous all-around athlete while growing up and he ended up earning a scholarship for Ole Miss University, which just so happened to be the team his father passionately supported. Archie went on to be a star college football player for the same university he and his dad had followed throughout Archie's childhood.

Heading into Archie's junior year, he went home for the summer to find his dad had taken his own life. Archie was the one who found his dead father and the film covered how this moment really impacted Archie's life. Archie's dad was not one to hug or say "I love you." Archie felt a deep sadness his father passed away, which left a void and painful reminder that his relationship with his dad wasn't as close as he would have liked it to have been. My interpretation of the events described in Archie's childhood seemed to drive him to be the best father he could be for his three boys. The film showed some great footage, from old home videos, of the three Manning boys' childhood. It chronicled the milestones their mom and dad did a great job of capturing.

When Archie was interviewed, he talked about how he didn't want to force his boys to play football, or any other sport for that matter. His goal was to always put the interests and needs of the boys first. It seemed as though Archie had such a great relationship with his boys and that they wanted to be just like him and play football. Archie made sure not to push the boys toward football and had a rule they couldn't play tackle football until they reached the 7th grade. Archie and Olivia also picked a school for their boys based on the academic reputation of the school, rather than the athletic reputation.

In the documentary, Peyton recalled a time when he was very young and was playing an organized sport. Peyton's dad observed his son being disrespectful to his coach through his body language and gestures. Peyton remembers later that day his dad drove him to his coach's house and Peyton had to apologize. This had quite an impact on Peyton and since that incident he, has always tried to be respectful to coaches and other authority figures.

Peyton and Eli are the two sons who are now celebrities in the world of professional football, but it was interesting to learn more about the oldest son, Cooper, who is not as well-known as his brothers. Cooper was passionate about football and he and Peyton ended up playing on the same high school football team when Cooper was a senior and Peyton was a sophomore. They had a successful season and Cooper ended up earning a scholarship to play at Ole Miss University, which was the same school his dad stared at years ago.

Before Cooper's playing career at Ole Miss began, he learned he had a condition called spinal stenosis and would have to give up playing football forever. His condition was serious enough that if he played, he was only one hit away from possible paralysis. It was amazing to see Cooper talk about this memory so many years later, which was quite emotional for him. Cooper went on to say although he loved football, it was the locker room and the bus rides home, he would forever miss. Cooper's experience is evidence of the power of sports to unify and bond teammates, as mentioned in the last chapter.

One final segment of the documentary that stood out was the film's account of Peyton going through the process of choosing which college he would attend. Archie was such a legend at Ole Miss most people in the state of Mississippi just assumed Archie would steer Peyton toward accepting a scholarship to play at Ole Miss University. Peyton was one of the top quarterback recruits in the country coming out of high school and he had over 100 offers to play football and earn a full scholarship at various universities.

Years later, Peyton said that if his dad had told him to attend Ole Miss he probably would have done so because of the way he idolized his dad. Instead, Archie let Peyton make his own decision and he decided to accept a scholarship from the University of

Tennessee. After the decision was made public, there was severe backlash and Ole Miss fans accused Archie of treason, called him a traitor and sent hate mail to both he and Peyton. I admire how Archie let Peyton make his own decision and am impressed by the way he and Peyton handled the adversity that came along with this situation.

I have always marveled at the way the entire Manning family presents themselves in the public eye. This family always seems to handle themselves with class and composure, even when confronted with adversity. For years, I have noticed Peyton and Eli's post-game interviews where they are always dressed nice are very polite and well-spoken, even when fielding questions from challenging reporters.

Now that I've had the opportunity to see the documentary, and have more insight as to how the Mannings raised their boys, I'm not surprised that they all turned out to be very respectable people. I noticed many of the elements we have covered in this book. Parallels include the Mannings having pure intentions as parents, cultivating intrinsic motivation in their children and teaching and guiding their kids toward learning valuable life lessons through sports.

Other Notable Role Models

It is important for parents to point out sports figures who are in the public eye that represent themselves in a positive light to our children. Hopefully, this strategy will encourage our kids to gravitate toward some of the athletes who stand out because of positive behavior as opposed to negative behaviors that tend to be displayed by the media.

Jordan Spieth, who I mentioned earlier, is also an athlete who had a real breakthrough year in 2015. He won two major tournaments and a total of five tournaments in October of that year. Spieth represents himself with class and grace and seems to have a level of maturity well beyond his years. I watched some of Spieth's interviews after he won the 2015 Masters and was blown away by the composure this 21-year-old displayed in handling questions. In studying some of Jordan's background when researching this book, I gained a real appreciation for his family and how they seemed to raise him.

Jordan's 14-year-old sister, Ellie, has autism and Jordan is very close with her and is one of her biggest supporters. I've heard him share Ellie's struggles help to keep him grounded and focused, as well as keep the game of golf in the proper perspective. He knows that no matter how much adversity he may encounter in his profession, it doesn't compare to some of the struggles his sister goes through every day. This realization helps to keep him humble.

I have also gained an appreciation for the mental toughness that Spieth exhibits even during moments of the most intense pressure in his sport. When asked how he remains so cool in the midst of high pressure situations, he said he tries to draw upon past experiences and stay in the moment. He focuses on what's within his control and if he has an untimely bad shot, he quickly forgets it, or moves past it, because dwelling on that won't help him to execute his next shot. Also, worrying about what his opponents are doing can only distract him from the task at hand. This sounds easier said than done, but watching how he responded in pressure-packed moments during his outstanding 2015 season, leads me to believe he practices what he preaches.

Stephen Curry was another high profile athlete who was in the spotlight a lot in 2015. Since he entered the NBA, Steph has always been a really good player but he took it to another level during the 2015 season. He won the regular season Most Valuable Player (MVP) award and his team went on to win the NBA finals. What strikes me about Steph is he really seems to value family and he's not afraid to let it be known. He is playing in a league where unfortunately, it's publicized far too often about how many players have had multiple children with different woman. This is not the case for all NBA players, but there have been enough high profile situations brought to light that have certainly hurt the reputation of the sport.

It's refreshing to see a player like Steph Curry have his mom, dad, brother, wife and daughter in the crowd supporting him at most of his games. During one of the NBA finals games, there was some debate stirred in the media as to whether Steph should have brought his two- year-old daughter, Riley, to his post-game interviews. Many thought Riley was distracting and took away from the integrity of the interviewing process. I heard from some sports talk radio hosts it would not be acceptable for most individuals to bring their children to work, so why is it any different for a professional sports player. I admired Steph for sticking to his convictions and allowing his daughter to be a part of the process. This was Steph's way of spending a little extra time with his daughter. It was refreshing to see this, especially in a sport where too many players make headlines for not paying enough attention to family.

The final athlete I'll highlight is Tim Tebow. At the time of writing this book, Tim is no longer playing professional sports but I've long admired him for his conviction and his passion. Tebow is arguably one of the best college quarterbacks to ever play, based on his track record of winning championships and his role in leading his teams. Tebow has always been somewhat controversial because he is very religious and some people are turned off by athletes who flaunt their beliefs. Whether you agree with his beliefs or not, it's hard to argue that Tebow possesses energy and passion and how infectious that can be in a team setting.

Tebow did not have nearly the level of success at the professional level that he did in college. He did have one year in the NFL, during the 2011 season, where he led his team to the playoffs and a victory over the Pittsburgh Steelers. Tebow never had the same skillset of other quarterbacks who went on to be successful in the NFL, but that year he was a true leader on that team who led by example and believed in his teammates. The Broncos had a number of victories that year that were not pretty at all. There were times that Tebow didn't play well for three quarters but he rose to the occasion and made key plays that led to his team winning the game when it mattered most. I love pointing out to kids I coach the qualities that Tebow possesses, in hopes they will want to emulate these qualities as they get older.

Coaches that Set the Right Example

Coaches have the enormous responsibility of leading young people who are very impressionable. As I've mentioned throughout this book, youth sports coaches are often volunteering their time to help because no one else will. Coaches might also have a real passion for wanting to influence the lives of kids through sports. In most cases, they "wing it" without having any real training or development. These coaches, just like kids, are influenced by what they see from coaches in the spotlight or maybe the influences from their past coaches guide their thoughts and actions while coaching.

When I think of the term "old school coach, "the image of Paul "Bear" Bryant comes to mind. I once read the book "The Junction Boys," which gave good insight to the approach of one of the most successful coaches of all time. He wanted to toughen up those he coached and some of the stories in the book describe how his teams practiced on dry, dusty field didn't get water breaks in extreme heat and some athletes played through broken bones.

Bear Bryant wasn't the only coach from this era who felt a coach's role was to toughen players up and run practices and games in a very militant manner. This approach was much more prevalent in that era than it is today, but the media still highlights coaches of today, who might still hold on to some of those old fashioned ideals. A couple of years ago, an incident surfaced where the Rutgers men's basketball coach made the news because a video showed him berating his players in practice by throwing basketballs at them and taunting them with vulgar language and homophobic slurs. This coach ended up getting fired as a result of this behavior, but unfortunately there have been other similar instances uncovered where high level coaches have behaved in an inappropriate manner.

Just as it's important for kids to seek out positive role models in the athlete's, part-time coaches should also be selective in choosing what leadership style they choose to emulate. Tony Dungy is a high profile former coach, who I have admired for a long time. Dungy had a long coaching career and had a lot of success at the NFL level, which culminated in his Indianapolis Colts team winning the Super Bowl in 2007. Tony started working as an analyst, shortly after retiring from coaching, so he still has influence and is heavily involved in the game of football.

Tony was a strong leader for his teams without feeling compelled to use profanity or scream to command his team's attention. He cared just as much about developing the person/athlete, as he did about his win/loss record. Professional football can be a very cutthroat business, where if you don't win you won't be around very long. Yet Tony was able to have a very long coaching career by focusing on developing strong relationships with his players. A number of Dungy's former players still speak of their old coach with great reverence. He also developed his former assistant coaches to the point where they've been able to become head coaches at the professional and collegiate level. Dungy is also the national spokesperson for an organization called "All-Pro Dad," that is designed to get fathers more involved in their kids' lives through monthly breakfast meetings and other family-friendly activities.

Mike Matheny is another coach who I really admire. I mentioned Mike earlier in the book, and what I like about him is he had a long playing career in the Major Leagues where he played at the highest and most competitive level. Yet when he retired, and he was asked to coach his son's youth baseball team, he agreed to do so only if the parents agreed to some of his demands. He set clear expectations and stated if he was to coach the team he would ensure the whole experience was about the kids and all outside distractions would be eliminated.

Parents agreed to his terms, which included just clapping and no talking or yelling when the kids were playing. He did not make winning the focal point, but rather developing the character of the kids and teaching them life lessons through the sport he loved. This was his number one priority for the kids. Even though winning wasn't the most important thing for the teams he coached, his teams had a lot of success based on measuring success the traditional way through the won/loss record. Mike has since taken over as the manager for the St. Louis Cardinals, where he has had consistent success since taking over this role.

The final coach I'll recognize became a household name during a successful run leading the Little League team he coached to the Little League World Series. Dave Belisle coached the Cumberland Americans to the Little League World Series in Williamsport, Pennsylvania in 2014. After a heartbreaking one run loss, that ended his team's chances of being Little League World Series champions, Belisle gave a post-game impassioned speech to the boys he coached. His speech was captured and went viral on sports media outlets, as well as on YouTube, where it gained a tremendous amount of views.

Belisle told the boys he loved them and shared with the team just how proud he and the entire town of Cumberland were. He went on to say, "You had the whole place jumping. You had the whole state jumping. You had New England jumping. You had ESPN jumping. Because you want to know why? They like fighters. They like sportsmen. They like guys that don't quit. They like guys that play the right way".

Belisle's inspirational speech made the boys realize that losing the game didn't make the whole process meaningless and there were so many positives to take from the experience. I would recommend looking up the speech on YouTube to witness this proud youth sports coach leave a lasting impression on the young boys he led. Belisle was not a professional coach but a full-time salesman, who coached youth sports for the love of the game. You'd be hard pressed to find someone who does a better job of embodying what youth sports is all about.

When our kids thoroughly enjoy sports, they will be in a great position to experience the many benefits that will serve them throughout their lifetime. They'll more than likely develop into fans of college and professional sports teams. Although they may want to put some of their favorite players on a pedestal, we can teach them no one is perfect and we want to be careful not to idolize players. There might be a time when their favorite player makes the news for an inappropriate action. This can be a big let-down for a kid to find out his or her favorite player isn't perfect. Instead, parents can be intentional about the attributes we feel standout in athletes and coaches, who are in the spotlight, to provide constant reinforcement of the right and wrong ways for our kids to s represent themselves in sports and in life.

9

Bringing It All Together

Although I am passionate about sports, by no means do I think participation in sports is the be-all and end-all necessary to raise good kids. My family's philosophy is to give kids the ability to try all sorts of different activities ranging from music and the arts to Boys and Girl Scouts. I do feel there is a place in every child's development for youth sports because of many of the reasons I've mentioned throughout this book.

As long as we enroll our children in sports with their best interests in mind and our intentions are pure, the kids will have a better chance of enjoying themselves throughout their years of playing sports. When parents think of their child as their "meal ticket," and have aspirations to have their kids play professional sports or earn a college scholarship, that the pressure starts to creep in and most likely will lead to kids wanting to quit at an early age. The paradox is just about all of the successful sports figures I've mentioned, have grown up being intrinsically motivated, or driven to succeed ,because their parents didn't force them to do anything they didn't want to do. This approach helped these players develop a love for their sport and could be a reason they're successful.

We also covered how specialization in one sport is becoming more of the norm, which often causes participation to dip because the experience becomes more of a job for the kids and they no longer find it fun. The push to specialize is another interesting paradox because we also covered examples of coaches who want to recruit kids who have played multiple sports because they tend to be better developed athletically, and are less prone to injury. Coaches who try to "sell" you on why your child needs to specialize in a sport so they don't fall behind, should pay attention to the athletes who reach the highest levels of success because they played multiple sports.

Once our children start having fun participating in sports, they'll be well on their way to a lifetime of enjoyment that can manifest itself into a desire to continue playing sports recreationally. This desire can also lead to children becoming lifetime sports fans. Once this foundation has been laid, sports can act as a great unifier by connecting them with former teammates and friends. Sports are also often used as an excuse to plan travel with family and friends and even increase the frequency of contact between those contacts.

We also know it's natural for kids to gravitate toward athletes they see on T.V. and may idolize them as heroes. Knowing this, we can also try to do our best to constantly point out the positives about the athletes who we feel embody the traits or attributes we'd like to see in our kids. Our guidance in this process is crucial to make sure they're not glorifying the wrong types of behaviors or actions.

Parents, who keep these principles and concepts in mind, while raising their kids, can use youth sports as a platform to enrich children's lives in their journey through their childhood. Including these strategies in a child's development process, helps to make the value they gain from youth sports less accidental and more intentional. You now know where I stand on the subject, and I encourage you to create an intentional plan that is customized for your own children. Following these strategies should help your family experience the Transformative Effect of Youth Sports while enriching the lives and enhance the development of the children that are so important to you.

ABOUT THE AUTHOR

J ason Kerrick has leveraged his leadership experience gained during his professional career along with his lifelong passion for sports to shape his philosophy of the role that youth sports plays throughout childhood development. He played numerous sports throughout his youth, coached and umpired collegiate intramurals and currently continues to coach many different youth sports. He has combined these experiences with leadership principles learned through 17 years of managing people to create actionable plans geared towards guiding and mentoring young athletes. Additionally, he enjoys spending his free time with his wife and two children. His work can be found on jasonkerrick. com as well as on Instagram and Twitter @jkerrick2977.

SOURCES

Chapter 1-

1. NPR.org- Poll by Robert Wood Foundation and the Harvard T.H. Chan School of Public Health "A Look at Sports & Health in America" by Scott Hensley 6/15/2015

2. A 2012 survey in CBS Moneywatch "8 Things you should know about sports scholarships" by Lynn O'Shaughnessy. Moneywatch 9/12/2012
3. Book "The Matheny Manifesto"

Chapter 2-

1. Childhood Obesity Basics- "Childhood Obesity" by Vincent Iannelli, M.D. Pediatrics Expert
2. Nfl.com- July of 2012 statistics given in support of the NFL Play 60 Initiative.
3. University of Illinois at Urbana-Champaign- "Children's brain development is linked to   physical fitness, research finds" September 16, 2010

Chapter 3

1. Book "The Matheny Manifesto"
2. Book "Why Less is More for   Well-Intentioned,
Overinvolved, Sports Parents". By Dr. John Tauer

Chapter 5-

1. Journal of Leadership and Organizational Studies "Sports
at Work" 2015

Chapter 6-

1. The Washington Post "Are Parents   ruining youth
sports? Fewer kids play amidst pressure" by Michael
Rosenwald
2. Forbes magazine "7 Billion Reasons Why the Youth Sports
Stadium Game Shows No Sign of Ending" by Bob Cook
3. Blog by Keith Van Horn- "Layups and Rebounds"
4. Titleist Performance Institute " Athlete First" by TPI
5. Parents Magazine "The Importance of Multiple Sports:
Stop Specializing in Sports So Early" by David Sparrow

Chapter 7-

1. Book "Flow" by Mihaly Csikszentmihalyi

Made in the USA
Monee, IL
04 January 2023

24550277R00079